SIKH
FORMS AND SYMBOLS

SIKH
Forms and Symbols

Edited by
MOHINDER   SINGH

MANOHAR
2000

First published 2000

© Mohinder Singh, 2000

ISBN 81-7304-310-8

Published by
Ajay Kumar Jain for
Manohar Publishers & Distributors
4753/23 Ansari Road, Daryaganj
New Delhi 110002

Typeset by
A J Software Publishing Co. Pvt. Ltd.
305 Durga Chambers
1333 D.B. Gupta Road
Karol Bagh, New Delhi 110005

Printed at
Rajkamal Electric Press
B 35/9 G T Karnal Road Indl Area
Delhi 110033

Dedicated to
the
Tercentenary of the
Khalsa

Contents

Foreword

In the realm of religion 'symbol' has a specific connotation. The origin of this term seems to go back to certain ancient usages of law according to which two parts of a ring, staff or tablet, when brought together, serve to identify guests (*terra hospitals*), messengers and partners. Thus the word came to signify 'treaty' and in the semitic ecclesiastical world stands for the common profession of faith and creed, instruments and acts through which faith was expressed.

In ordinary usage, a symbol is a 'thing regarded by general consent as naturally typifying, representing or recalling something (especially an idea or quality) by possession of analogous qualities or by association in fact or thought' (*Concise Oxford Dictionary*). Thus an ordinary symbol essentially signifies something else. A religious symbol, on the other hand, does not refer to something else. In fact, a reality appears in it—in 'the other of itself'. That reality is very much present in the symbol, though not fully exhausted by its appearance. Let us ponder over it by taking the example of 'unshorn hair' which is one of the important Sikh symbols. Keeping the hair intact, in the very form in which it has been bestowed upon us by Divine Nature signifies that we regard Divine Wisdom as infallible in contrast to human intellect which is subject to error as well as deceit. The hair thus became a symbol of that Divine Nature which is both present in it and finds expression through it. Tampering with hair, on any pretence, would tentamount to placing human intellect higher than Divine Wisdom. And that has been decreed as a grave sin in the Sikh faith.

The expression 'merely a symbol' deserves outright rejection, because it is always more than what it tangibly is. It essentially stands for the being, appearance and self-positioning of what it signifies. And therein lies its grandeur.

A symbol is neither a fetish nor an image for worship, although by virtue of what it signifies, it might become worshipable. '*Kirpan*' (the sword), which is a Sikh symbol becomes worshipable for it signifies *Shastra* Bhagwan, the Charge Divine. It becomes the manifestation of the Divine Dynamic.

'He designed the double-edged sword before
He created the Universe.'

Guru Gobind Singh: *Var Sri Bhagautiji ki*

The 'double-edged' sword here signifies the dual dynamics of creation and devastation which has simultaneously been active right from the very beginning. Thus this sword, in a way, becomes *Vestigia Dei*, the tangible manifestation of the transcendent creativity.

Charged with such fullness of significance, religious symbols acquire universal validity. They summon, evoke and provide meaning which is unbound by time, space and culture.

It is from such a point of view that religious symbols need to be valued. This collection of articles: 'Sikh Forms and Symbols' requires to be approached with like intent.

New Delhi   J.S. Neki

Editor's Note

Like all other living religions Sikhism too is facing fresh challenges as a result of worldwide dispersal of the Sikhs and the diaspora's anxiety to preserve distinct forms and symbols of their religious and cultural heritage. This has often resulted in serious debates and occasional conflicts with the host cultures. The issue of preserving hair and other Sikh symbols became a matter of serious concern when a Sikh friend from the United States addressed a letter to the Sikh intelligentsia in India, Punjabi translation of which was published in the popular Sikh daily *Akali te Pardesi* of 20 October 1926. In the letter the young friend explained his dilemma that as a devout Sikh he was not prepared to resolve the controversy by discarding his religious symbols as most of the Sikh pioneers had done when confronted with the hostile atmosphere in the host countries. At the same time this youngman was unable to find coherent reasons in support of the traditional symbols in an alien land. He prayed that the thinking Sikh minds help him come out of the *impasse*. Gyani Sher Singh took the initiative of circulating the English version of this letter to some eminent Sikh scholars of that time, such as Bhai Jodh Singh, Professor Teja Singh and Professor Gurmukh Nihal Singh to elicit their opinion.

The Sikhs, who constituted bulk of the army in India under the British rule, were supported and encouraged by the British rulers in maintaining distinct forms and symbols of their faith. When they were fighting on different European fronts in the British forces, the British commanders did not force Sikh soldiers to replace their turbans with hats. Because of the sacrifices Sikhs made in the two World Wars, the Government of Britain also allowed its British-Sikh officers to wear their traditional headgear. However, opposition to the turban came in Britain from rather unexpected quarters. In 1959 the Manchester Transport Department rejected the application of Mr. G.S. Sagar, a Sikh who applied for the position of a bus-conductor because of his insistence on wearing his traditional turban rather than the uniform cap prescribed by the transport authority. Refusal of job to Mr. G.S. Sagar led to a serious debate and controversy in Britain. Sagar asserted that wearing of the turban was an essential part of his religious beliefs. He further argued that if thousands of Sikhs, who had fought and died for the Empire on various fronts during the two World Wars, could wear their turbans why could he not do so. The transport authorities argued that if they made an exception in this case they could not enforce uniform rules on other employees.

On the face of it, the controversy seemed to be an employer's right to enforce rules with regard to employee's dress and latter's right to follow injunctions of his religion. But for a variety of reasons the arena of the struggle widened with the transport workers' union supporting the management rather than a fellow worker because of working-class whites' resentment against the dark skinned intruders. During more than seven years of fight on the issue Mr. Sagar not only received support from the Sikhs and the Sikh associations in the United Kingdom but also from the British councillors which resulted in the turban being accepted as a part of the prescribed dress by the transport authorities in Manchester in 1967.

There has been no problem after the settlement of the turban issue in Manchester and Wolverhampton, and Sikhs with their turban and symbols intact found respectable place in various establishments including the Police and the Army. However, the issue again came to the fore as a result of Calgary-based group of Royal Canadian Mounted Police (RCMP) veterans having filed a suit in a Federal Court challenging the constitutionality of changing the dress code regulations in force that allowed the Sikh officers to wear turbans instead of Stenton hats. The Sikhs again had to launch a fresh struggle and finally won the battle when the Canadian authorities accepted the turban as a part of the dress code of the RCMP

The entry of Gurbax Singh Malhi, the newly elected member of the Canadian Parliament, with his turban created history in the House of Commons in Canada. On being re-elected to the Canadian Parliament, Malhi created history of sorts by taking oath of office in the presence of the *Guru Granth Sahib* in June 1997.

While the Sikh diaspora in UK and Canada succeeded in getting official recognition for their religious symbols, a fresh controversy began in California, United States, over the issue of school children being denied to wear *kirpan*, one of the five symbols prescribed for the baptised Sikhs. After some initial setbacks the Sikh community succeeded in this case too—with the Senate passing a bill unanimously allowing the Sikh children to attend schools while wearing their traditional symbol of *kirpan*. Apart from public debate, the issue has been discussed at length in a scholarly essay by Professor Vinay Lal of the University of California, Los Angles which also is included in this volume.

At a time when Sikhism has become a world religion because of universal message of the Gurus and worldwide dispersal of its followers, it is important that the younger generation learns about its rich heritage of suffering and sacrifice and has determination to preserve distinct forms and symbols of its faith. On the occasion of the tercentenary of the creation of the Khalsa, we pay our tribute to the founder through this anthology on Sikh forms and symbols of the Sikh faith

I would like to thank Dr. J.S. Neki for his Foreword, the contributors and in particular Prof. Anurag Singh for the permission to reproduce Dr. Trilochan Singh's article in this volume.

New Delhi   MOHINDER SINGH
13 April 2000

Letter from a Sikh Friend
in America

Received your kind note last week accompanied by Professor Teja Singh's instructive letter, and the Khalsa College Magazine. I am sorry, I could not answer promptly because I was too busy. I thank you for your efforts to convince me about the necessity of forms and symbols in Sikhism, though they had a negative effect on me. This may not sound good to you, but if I tell you just the opposite only to please you, that will be harmful to me and a deceit to your efforts. However, you should not misunderstand me if I ask questions about Sikh religious symbols. My object is not a mere discussion or criticism, but a pure effort to find out the truth about them. If my object had been only to get rid of my hair I could very easily have done that without troubling anybody; as a majority of the Sikhs here do. To them it seems to be the easiest way, but it is a dirty trick. It is not only deceiving the parents or one's ownself but a great blow on the Sikh religion. They are misunderstood as Christian converts. Before doing that, if all of them got together and sincerely approached the Panth, the Panth would be obliged to mitigate their suffering or deny the truth. This might seem a foolish proposal, but it is not so. I am not trying to manufacture anything but they are my real inward feelings. I have met and heard from a great many of the Sikhs in America and Europe. Everybody faces the same problem, but nobody comes to discuss the matter with anybody at home. They say, 'People at home, who adhere to their Sikh principles in comfortable circumstances, will not try to understand us, but will take our criticism in an opposite way, because they do not know the conditions here, and instead of encouragement and relief they will try to make light of our difficulties.' This seems to be quite true. Those who send back their complaints and diverse convictions are considered to be weak-minded, affected by the ideas of Christianity, or rogues who want to enjoy beautiful girls after cutting off their hair. At any rate, all those who cut off their hair and go back in the same condition are supposed to be Christian converts, although they may be as far away from Christianity as any other Sikh, and in some cases even better Sikhs in spirit than the average Sikhs.

I have very little time at my disposal, so I may not be able to write to Professor Teja Singh very soon. I have read his article, his letter, and your letter very carefully. I find those things explained that don't need any explanation. I think I could have understood better if the Professor had only answered the questions I had asked in my letter. The article explains its object nicely in a general way, but it did not remove the suspicions that I had. You have said in your letter that the article was most convincing. It would have been exactly so to me if I had been at home. I will explain briefly how the article affects me. To me it is quite clear that Sikh forms and symbols are just the same as there are forms in other organizations. They are not essential for every Sikh in all circumstances. They are for the betterment of the Sikh Panth, but if they show any disadvantages, there is no harm in amending them. You will think that this is an opposite effect than the writer had designed the article for. In this article, Professor Sahib cites the examples of caste-system, cooking squares, and sacred threads, 'which', he says, 'were originally designed for some definite good purpose, but by the time of Sri Guru Nanak Dev they had become so old and corrupt that he asked the Hindus to renounce them'. Our forms had the same kind of origin as the above mentioned forms. Then, is there any guarantee against our symbols and forms getting so old that they will not remain fit for the purpose they were designed? (Forms and symbols are determined for the pure necessity of the organizations which are a part of the religion. These forms have at least no defects if they don't have much more advantages to make the followers more efficient in performing their mission. But when these forms don't serve that purpose, they are no better than mere local or racial symbols that must be abandoned to avoid division and exclusiveness.)

In America, the idea of letting the hair grow as they naturally do seems to be more unreasonable and gewgaw than the idea of 'eating squares' was in the days of Guru Nanak. It seems no better than a racial and local difference and it certainly is a blockade against social intercourse. It is thought by the people to be as primitive as when human beings roamed naked in the jungles. To the people around it is a sign of ignorance. (You will answer that we should behave better so that people should know our ability, but that is not the point I am driving at.) Why should they not save him that trouble? Same is the case with iron ring. Nobody searches for our sternness (for which it is meant), but the show of iron ring affects him the way we are affected when we see tavit, tuna, jogi's earrings or the idols.

Perfectly understood that religion is not only an individual concern, but it is an organization of individuals of the same ideas who try to search for truth in one way. As human nature has sentiments, emotions, and imaginations so these organizations adopt some forms to assure the continuity of expression. These forms are not bondage to individuals but pleasure and pride. They are not dead but a living index of his ideals. Those who do not adopt these forms cannot be the part of the organization because those who cry against all forms cannot contribute in any meaningful way to the well-being of society. I know how our forms and symbols originated, how nicely they have worked so far. But I think they need some reforms now. I feel guilty to say that, I think that we cannot follow some ideals freely and firmly, if we do not know exactly what they are and if we cannot discuss and reform them when we find fault with them. An ignorant fellow like me has nothing to say in such important matters, but he will never come out of ignorance if he thinks that he has no say in connection therewith. Professor Sahib says that our forms are just the same type as the forms in military and salvation army. I certainly agree to that, and I am proud that Sikh Panth will always keep some forms. In military the forms are for some definite purpose, and they are so designed that the soldiers in them can be most efficient. Nobody in those forms can be handicapped in the purpose for which they are designed. These forms are changed from time to time with the change of the environment. The invention of gunpowder cut out the brilliant and shiny uniforms of the soldiers and replaced the sword by rifle and pistol. If some armies now get the idea of keeping the same forms as red jackets, an axe, a sword and a shield, they will certainly have a hard time. The question of our sword is exactly the same. A soldier on leave is as good, as a soldier on duty. Living out of forms for a short time does not effect him any way.

Panth has as much power as Gurus had, why can it not make changes when it seems necessary? If the Christians had not reformed their Old Testament, there would have been very few Christians by this time. The only thing that restricts Sikhism from spreading is the strictness of the forms. No body here will grow hair even if he believes in every bit of Sikh philosophy. All the Gurus had been making changes in Sikh religion in their lifetime why should the Panth be deprived of this right? If the Panth does not find any need for change, it can make some allowances for those who go in different circumstances. We find the same kind of example in Sikh history. Some Sikhs were sent to Benaras by Guru Gobind Singh to study Hindu Theology but they were not required to follow in the same form as the other Sikhs.

When the forms are not quite indispensable why should the Sikh students suffer? If the Panth deems them necessary in Homeland at present, they can be adopted again just the same when the students return. Why an educated man is handicapped for mere forms. A soldier in trench should not have the same uniform and equipment as the one in aeroplane.

I have not been able to express myself clearly; please try to get what I mean and don't catch me on words, when you answer, please don't try to manufacture reasons to cut out my petty disbeliefs (we can find reasons for and against every subject that we happen to discuss) but try to think the way I do, and then find some relief for me. If you will give some reasons only for the sake of discussion, they will do me harm instead of any good. Please refer to my previous letters and see what I am driving at. I think that you know all the difficulties that Sikh students have to face, so I don't feel the need to explain them. I am not discouraged by the hardships I have to face, the obstacles even strengthen my determination, but why I should show my sternness and get handicapped if it is not absolutely necessary, I cannot understand.

Sikh Symbols

TEJA SINGH

The principle of organization is a part of the Sikh religion. A Sikh is not only to look to his individual character but is also to shoulder his responsibilities as a part of the corporate body of the Panth. This is evident from the form of congregational worship and the daily prayer of Sikhs, wherein the Sikh invokes after God, all the ten Gurus and the deeds of those great Sikhs who have suffered for the Panth. It brings before his mind the present organic life of the community, with its different associations and meeting-places scattered everywhere, thus steeping himself every day in the association of those who constitute the past and present history of the Panth. This institution entails certain additional disciplinary outfits in the shape of baptismal forms and vows, which are often misunderstood. People cannot easily understand how it is that, while in *Asa di Var* the Guru ridicules certain forms and symbols, the Sikh religion has yet got its own which it considers as a regular part of its constitution.

It is true that if religion were only a matter of individual concern, there would be no need of forms or symbols. But religion, as taught by the Gurus, is a force that not only ennobles individuals but binds them together to work for nobility in the world. And an organization is means of enlarging the possibility, scope, and effectiveness of this work. In order that an organization may itself work effectively, it is necessary that the individuals involved with it should be able to keep up their attachment to the cause and a sufficient amount of enthusiasm for it. It is, however, a patent fact that men by their nature are so constituted that they cannot keep their feelings high-strung for a long time at a stretch. Reaction is inevitable, unless some means are devised to ensure the continuity of exertion. This is where discipline comes in. It keeps up the spirit of individuals against relaxation in times of trial and maintains their loyalty to the cause even in moments of distress. This discipline, or what is called *esprit de corps*, is secured by such devices as flags and drills and uniforms in armies and certain forms and ceremonies in religion. Uniformity is an essential part of them. They create the necessary enthusiasm by appealing to the imagination and sentiment, and work for it in moments of depression. They are a real aid to religion, which is essentially a thing of sentiment. Man would have no need for them were he only a bundle of intellectual and moral sense; but as he also has sentiments and imagination without which the former qualities would be inoperative, he cannot do without articulating his ideas and beliefs in some forms appropriate to the sentiment. These forms must not be dead but a living index of his ideal, awakening in him vivid intimations of the personality that governs his religion. They should be related to his inner belief as words are to their meanings, tears to grief, smiles to happiness, and a tune to a song. It is true that sometimes words become meaningless; when we no longer heed their sense or the language to which they belong, they becomes dead. It is true, that sometimes tears and smiles are only cloaks for hypocrisy, and a tune, a mere meaningless jingle. But there is no denying the fact that when their inner meaning is real, and we are sincere about it, they do serve as very helpful interpreters. Forms are the art of religion. Like art of nature, these forms impose certain limitations on the ideal, but at the same time they make the ideal more real and workable for general use.

Sometimes, however, when the forms are determined, not by necessity of uniformity, which is so essential to discipline, but by the local or racial causes, they narrow the applicability of the ideal, create division and exclusiveness where as they should have helped men to unite. When the spirit in which they had been originally conceived dies out, they become mere handicaps to religion, and the people who use them would be well advised to abandon them. A telescope certainly helps the sight in looking at things far in the heaven, but when its lens becomes so defective that instead of helping the naked eye it proves an actual hindrance in its way, then the telescope must be put aside. It was such forms that Guru Nanak asked the Hindus to discard. The custom of taking food within cooking squares must have begun in the desire to eat in clean places, which is very desirable. But by the time of the Guru, it had become merely a sign of exclusiveness and had no reference to cleanliness. Similarly the caste-system must have grown out of the economic necessity to carry on their vocations differently, but it became condemnable when it tied down certain people to a lower social position, simply because their forefathers had once been forced to submit to it. The sacred thread was also like a symbol of exclusiveness. Such forms only seared the spirit of religion in India, and alienated the people from God. It was right, therefore, that the Guru should advise the people to destroy customs which made them forget God and set up barriers between man and man.

But the Sikh forms were not conceived in a spirit of exclusiveness, or as something essential to the spiritual advancement of the individual soul. They were simply appointed to serve as aids to the preservation of the corporate life of the community, and any man who likes to serve humanity through the Sikh Panth can wear them. It is possible for a man to love God and cultivate his individual soul without adopting these forms but if he wants to work in a systematic manner not only for his own advancement but for the good of others as well as in the company of Sikhs, he must adopt these disciplinary forms of the organization. It is possible for a single wrestler to acquire bodily strength equal to that of four soldiers in uniform, but this cannot be used as an argument against the formation of armies and the use among them of uniforms and other such things for the promotion of joint action. If the same wrestler were to train and eastablish a band of stout men like himself for some set purpose, he would see that certain forms and signs, which he had originally worn as his simple requirements, begin to appear on his followers dresses too—not as useless gewgaws, but helping maintain their *esprit de corps* and a pride in their work. Similarly Sikhs, who are the soldiers of Guru Gobind Singh and whose religion is surcharged with his personality, find the uniform worn and ordained by him as a real help in playing their part as units of the Panthic organization.

This help comes from the appeal made to sentiment by the process of association and not through any inherent efficacy of the forms themselves. This association is not with places or things, but with an ever-living personality that itself is a symbol of the Highest Personality. As is God, so is the Guru: and as is the Guru so must be the follower. Wearing long drawers ensuring briskness of movement in times of action and serving as an easy underwear at times of rest, an iron ring on his right arm as a sign of sternness and constraint; and a sword by his side as an instrument of defence and as an emblem of power and dignity, the Guru presented an impressive picture of a simple but disciplined soldier. He, however, combined in him the saintliness of the old *rishis* with the sternness and strength of a knight. Therefore, like his predecessors, he kept long hair, which the world over has always been associated with saintliness. A comb was a simple necessity for keeping the hair clean and tidy. These were the forms with which the Sikhs were invested at the time of their baptism, in order to look exactly like their Master, as they were required to behave exactly like him.

A study of the history of the Sikhs down the ages till the present, would reveal how effectively these baptismal forms, with the accompanying vows, have aided the members of the community in keeping themselves united and their ideals unsullied even in times of the greatest trial. While keeping the Sikhs associated with their Guru and maintaining his spirit among them, they have not produced any narrowing effect on their beliefs and modes of worship. Rather, as history tell us, changes for the worse have always synchronized with the want of insistence on the baptismal vows. This was in the days of the Sikh rule, when luxury and power tempted our people to consider the vows to be too demanding for them. They lost their identity as Sikhs and became as superstitious about God and His worship as they had been before the time of the Guru. With the modern revival the Sikhs have found themselves again, and with the old faith in the efficacy of the baptismal vows they still believe that God is one and that there is no worship more pleasing to Him than the heartfelt singing of His hymns. All worship and ceremony, whether in temple or at home, whether on birth, marriage, or death, consists of nothing else but praying and chanting hymns. Could anything be simpler?

Some people while admitting the necessity of some forms in religion do not approve of the particular forms in vogue and want the Panth to do away with them or invent some new ones in their place, which may be more suitable to the modern conditions of the society. This is a mere caprice, imported from the secular spheres of life, of ever-changing fashions. They ignore the universal fact that in religion whatever has once been accepted as an integral part of its constitution cannot be changed or dispensed with without changing or dispensing with the religion itself. This difference between social fashions and religious form is due to the fundamental differences between the natures of their origin. Fashions originate with different generations each of which has got an equal authority with respect to others; therefore no one generation can bind another in the observance of a particular fashion. Each generation is competent enough to invent its own mode of dress or behaviour. But in religion all obligations originate from its founder whose authority cannot be set aside except by himself or by a successor wielding equal authority jointly with him. In Sikhism any one of the ten Gurus, being equal with the others, was fully qualified to change or modify any rule set down by his predecessors; but after the tenth Guru, the supreme authority was divided and came to rest with the Panth and the collective teachings of the Gurus. The Panth is Guru only in conjunction with the teaching, and cannot be said to be the sole arbiter of its destiny. No generation of Sikhs, therefore, is competent enough to supercede the authority of the word or any genuine dictum handed down by the Gurus.

Then is there no possibility of reform in religion? Yes, there is. You can reform the doctrines and the practices obtaining at a particular time by removing the unauthorized accretions which have gathered round the original core through the ignorance of the followers, but in each case you will have to show that you are not removing anything original, but only the unnecessary interruption made by others without the Founder's consent. The Sikhs, in the course of their recent reforms, have done away with such observances as the *shradhs*, *sutak*, *janeu,* etc., because they were able to show by referring to the original sources that these were unauthorized accretions and that Sikhism had nothing to do with them. But they cannot similarly effect reforms to the Holy Granth, or make any additions to it from the writings of the modern saints and holy men, although by doing so they may be apparently, following the examples of the Gurus in making the Book more comprehensive and up-to-date. Similarly they cannot add a new Guru to the list of the original ten, nor withdraw their allegiance from any one of them. The position of the Sikh baptism and the baptismal forms is also equally uncompromising.

All the care that was needfed was taken by the Gurus in order not to encumber their religion with unnecessary forms, but the few that they did find necessary to incorporate in the scheme of their religion are an essential part of the Sikhs' religious outfit, and they can in no case dispense with them without going out of the pale of Sikhism. You may say that they are not as important as the belief in one God and other spiritual doctrines. But important they certainly are; and their importance, as shown already, lies in the help they provide in the maintenance of the Panthic organization, which is an essential part of Sikhism.

Baptism and Symbols in Sikhism

BHAI JODH SINGH

Before attempting to give a reply I should like to state the position clearly and briefly. The central idea in Sikh religion is the destruction of *Haumai* and thus knowing *Raza* which would become the guide of our life. This could be achieved by perfect obedience to the Guru, association with *Sadh sangat* and repetition of Name. A person as he comes to the Guru is not baptised at once. He becomes an Amritdhari only when he is able to fulfil certain vows which he takes at the time of baptism. It is then that along-with other vows he is asked to keep his hair uncut and wear the other four *Kakar*. If, after that he shaves his hair he is called *patit*, but if he omits to wear any of other four *Kakar* he is merely a *tankhaia*. There is thus a fundamental difference between the wearing of *kesh* and the remaining four *Kakar*.

The whole difficulty arises from the fact that people are given *amrit* before they are fit to receive it. Your friend appears to think that it is easier to be a Sikh in spirit than to keep the Sikh form of wearing the hair uncut. To me it appears, on the other hand, that keeping one's hair uncut is easier than following the spirit of Sikhism in our everyday life. Will one who really believes 'that whatever He does is for the best' for a moment think that he could improve the human form designed by the Maker by cutting off a living portion of it, viz., the hair. Keeping the hair uncut to me is the natural and outer manifestation of that spirit of *Razi Bar Raza* that is working within.

It is not a form that is superimposed but it is a form that grows from the seed that is sown within. I know of at least one great European thinker, Tolstoy by name, who says that the highest religion yet discovered by man is submission to His Will, and strange to say that this great thinker and writer gave up cutting his hair and beard. This is the meaning that I attach to keeping the hair uncut.

As for your friend's other contentions, I don't want to discuss them in detail. The Panth has no right to order a change in the fundamental principles, nor is the Panth the Guru in the sense in which your friend takes it. A true Sikh's first concern is obedience to the Guru. By that the object of his life is fulfilled. Such an obediance alone is of account, the rest is all the prattle of ego. Learning and wealth are not the objects he hankers after. He could sacrifice everything for the sake of the Guru. But that could be done only when one has realized the value of the Guru's Word. Ordinary men like myself deny him a thousand times everyday to live our life of *Haumai* and in spite of a show of great learning and a heap of material comforts we go empty-handed from this world.

Importance of *Kesh*

BAWA HARKISHAN SINGH

To my mind the letter of our friend from America raises two distinct questions: the disadvantages and difficulties that Sikh students face abroad, and the question of the justification of *kesh* in general. These two need not be mixed up. At the same time we should remember that disadvantages and difficulties exist for the Sikhs even at home, though in a smaller degree, and that doubts about the justification of *kesh* are sometimes voiced here as well. Honest doubt commands respect, while expression of doubt, intended as a convenient translation for leaving the fold, is not worthy and cannot be argued away.

As far as the difficulties of sincere, believing young men abroad are concerned, they will be lessened as the status of India and the Indians abroad improves. It is also necessary to provide a social environment for Sikh young men, where they may remain in touch with their own traditions and replenish their enthusiasm for Sikhism. A Students' Home, a Gurdwara, or a Social Club, which will be the best instrument, depends upon the conditions obtaining in different places.

As for the general question of the justification of *kesh*, my humble sudy and reflection has led me to the conclusion that our Master, Sri Guru Gobind Singh has, in his wisdom laid down certain simple rules of conduct for our guidance and we should therefore obey such rules. They are useful, they are reasonable, but that is not the primary reason for my accepting them. I accept them primarily because it is His binding. Sikhism does not claim to be founded on the 'dry light of reason' alone; emotion and sentiment are real potent factors in Sikhism. Reason is not discarded, rather, our aim is disciplined emotion and enlightened sentiment.

The moral quality of the Guru's teachings brings conviction to my reason, and I accept Him as my Master with confidence and faith.

Therefore, in such matters as the *kesh*, I do not feel the need of questioning. I do not approve of the practice of certain simple-minded people of arguing about the ordinary utility and the medical properties of *kesh*. Do they mean to say that if it were proved that the *kesh* confer no advantages then the Sikhs would give them up? The *kesh* are a help to the organization, but that is, again, not the primary reason for our wearing them.

I am of the firm opinion that the real reason for our wearing the *kesh* is an attachment to the personality and ideals of Guru Gobind Singh. What is necessary is not a campaign for propagating the uses and advantages of *kesh*, but an effort to reinforce the love for the Guru in the hearts of Sikh youth. When the sap dries, the leaves and the branches droop.

To sincere believing youngmen, whether here or abroad, who are troubled by honest doubt, I would humbly suggest, 'Get nearer the Guru's radiant and energizing personality through *Gurbani*, through reflection, and through prayer, for that is how doubt is best dispelled.'

For an exposition about *kesh* and other Sikh symbols which help our organization I would refer you to the excellent article of Prof. Teja Singh recently published by the Sikh Tract Society, Lahore. I have not entered into this aspect of the question here, for I do not believe that, that is the basic reason of our wearing the *kesh*. We should boldly and honestly take our stand on the fundamental attachment to the personality of Guru Gobind Singh.

The Sikh Symbols

GURMUKH NIHAL SINGH

The question about the sanctity of the Sikh symbols is gradually pre-occupying the minds of the thinking people of the community, though the Sikh masses are in no mood yet to entertain it. They regard their symbols as sacrosanct and any one who dares to question their sanctity is at once dubbed as a heretic. It is impossible for them to believe that the person who discards the symbols can still retain any love or respect for the Gurus or faith in the Sikh tenets. Every now and then they are shocked to hear that a young man has given up keeping long hair. They work themselves into a furious rage over the event but do nothing to probe into the causes of such an action. As a matter of fact this attitude of the Sikh masses makes it impossible to discuss the question frankly or thoroughly and yet it is obvious that the whole future of the Sikh community and the progress and spread of Sikhism are indissolubly bound to it. I request all those who are interested in the advancement of the Sikhs to give up the alarmist and unthinking attitude on this question of the symbols and ponder deeply over it to discover a satisfactory solution.

Symbols have played and still continue to play an important part in the Indian life. The best of Indian art is symbolic and millions of Indians worship God through the use of symbols—some of which are exceedingly crude and ugly. The use of symbols is necessary to carry abstract ideas to backward and ignorant people. Even the language and script of primitive people are symbolic and pictorial as in the case of the Chinese. The greatest difficulty with symbols is that with use they cease to be mere symbols; they become identified with the objects which they represent. The idol instead of representing God becomes God itself.

It has been pointed out that our symbols are not religious and therefore do not take us away from God. As far as the worship of God is concerned it is pure and unadulterated. Our God is a formless one. He is *Nirankar*. Our symbols are badges: they are like soldiers' uniform which mark off the initiated disciples of Guru Gobind Singh from those of the followers of other saints; and that the symbols of a Sikh remind him of the duties he owes to God, the Panth and man as the uniform reminds the wearer of his obligations to the king, army and the country. An analogy is a dangerous method in the hands of the uninitiated. It must always be remembered that an analogy is not a proof; similarity does not necessarily imply identity. Uniform is something that is temporary—it gets soiled and dirty. It can be changed and taken off temporarily or permanently. Surely Sikh symbols are not of this kind. And, moreover, Sikh symbols are after all not so unique as some of us imagine them to be. In south India there are many brahmins who keep a high *choti* and some who do not shave the hair of the head at all. I know of some Hindus who consider it as incumbent on them to keep long hair as do the Sikhs. And it is not very long ago that the Hindus used to be identified by their long hair. Hindus of one sect are often distinguished from those of another sect by the nature and form of the caste mark on the forehead. The Hindus of the three higher castes are differentiated from the *Shudras* by the wearing of the sacred thread. It is not necessary to multiply instances, they are given in abundance in our sacred scriptures.

There are some ingenious persons among us who, like the scholastics of the Middle Ages, have used their learning to invent curious arguments to justify the keeping of long hair. Some have tried to justify them on scientific grounds, as a protection against the sun and electric shocks. I know very little science, but my scientific friends tell me that keeping head tied up, as we Sikhs do, without any arrangement for ventilation is not only unscientific but positively injurious. And it is only habit that makes us put up with long hair and turban during the summer months. Some have requisitioned the services of history to demonstrate the necessity of keeping long hair as if anything that existed in the past was necessarily good. There are some who point to pictures of the sixteenth, seventeenth and eighteenth century Englishmen to prove the advantages of keeping long hair, little knowing that the hair seen in the pictures are not hair at all but wigs that were used by fashionable men in England during those days. And there are persons, educated men among us, who have discovered the most convincing proof in the story of Samson and Delilah as given in the Bible. Such arguments instead of helping us make us look ridiculous in the eyes of intelligent men.

Let us admit once for all that utility is the only test in cases of this kind. As long as symbols continue to serve a useful purpose in the life of the community, as long as they do not degenerate into mere forms but are instincts with meaning and life, and as long as they are kept alive and do not act as a drag on the onward march of the community, so long they have a right to exit; otherwise the sooner they are discarded the better it is for the well-being of the community. And the leaders have to keep a constant vigil to see that the symbols do not become a dead weight and are not in any way injurious to the development of the community.

The services that our symbols have rendered to us are unique. *Kesh* and *kirpan* especially have been a God-send to us. Without them we could not have lived through the terrible times through which we have passed ever since our birth. If we have escaped strangulation, if we still retain our individuality and identity, if we still have a spark of life in us it is largely due to the existence of these two symbols amidst us. The obligation to keep long hair made it impossible for weak-minded, comfort-loving persons to accept Sikhism and it made those who had already become Sikhs braver and hardier than before. If we had given up wearing long hair during the terrible times that followed the death of Guru Gobind Singh and had taken shelter in Hindu homes to escape Muslim persecution we would have soon forgotten the sublime teachings of the Gurus and would have drifted back to the superstitious practices from which the Gurus had extricated us. We were saved—those who were brave enough not to succumb to the temptation of a quiet life of comfort—from this tragedy by our long hair. The obligation to keep long hair took us away to the jungles; our *kirpans* helped us to protect ourselves. The jungles of the Punjab became the home of the persecuted brave Sikhs and there they lived ideal Sikh lives, which have proved a constant source of inspiration to those who have come after them. That is why *kesh* became so dear to the Sikhs; that is why men like Bhai Taru Singh preferred to suffer the tortures of the persecutors and allowed their bodies to be mangled and minced rather than to part with their long hair. He would be a foolish man indeed who would counsel the community to discard lightly the *kesh* when they have been of tremendous service to the community. Sikhism lived through its symbols during the period of Mughal persecution and it is these symbols that have kept us united and have given us the spirit which is the envy of the members of other communities in India.

Our symbols indeed have been of tremendous service to us and it is hardly possible to exaggerate their past utility. Our long hair has preserved our identity; our *kirpan* has maintained our life, property, and honour, our *kara* has taught us the value of upright, self-controlled, stern and disciplined life; our *kachha* has provided us with a convenient dress in summer and at night and with good underwear in winter; and the *kangha* has supplied the necessary instrument for keeping the hair clean and tidy. And they have constantly kept before our eyes the saintly figure of our Saviour and

Preceptor, Guru Gobind Singh and those of his inspired Sikhs, and have knit us together as nothing else would have done.

To what extent are these symbols of ours, living today? Are they still instilled with meaning and life, or have they become a dead weight retarding our progress? These are questions that deserve careful consideration at the hands of all well-wishers of the Panth.

The attitude of the masses towards the symbols is that of unquestioning reverence and of unthinking acquiescence. Many keep them as a matter of form. Few know their meaning and significance. Not 1 per cent of them, I am afraid, will be able to explain the purpose of wearing *kara* on the right arm. Yet, all the same, symbols are extremely useful to them. They remind them of their splendid inheritance and make them realize their unity and common entity. Take away the *kesh* and *kara*, *kachha* and *kirpan* and *kangha* from the Sikh masses today and within a few years they will lose their identity and will become hybrids—with one leg in one boat and the other in the second one—worshipping the Hindu idols and the Holy Granth at one and the same time. As long as the Sikh masses remain uneducated, as long as they are not discerning enough to grasp the lofty teachings of the Gurus unaided, they must continue to need the symbols. It is only through symbols, through following narrowly, without swerving even by a hair's breadth in the footsteps of the Gurus and of the Sikhs like Bhai Taru Singh, Bhai Mani Singh and others, that they can learn the true way of religion and reach God.

But what about the educated classes? Do they need them in the same way and to the same extent as the uneducated masses? I know many of them are capable of understanding, appreciating and following the highest teachings of the Gurus without the use of symbols, but even they cannot afford to discard them. They should not do anything to cut themselves off from their less educated brethren. They must remember that they have a duty to perform towards them. They owe it to the Gurus, the Panth and God to work amongst them and for their upliftment. And it must not be forgotten that they can only serve them and uplift them, if they go amongst them as one of them and in the form and appearance in which they can accept them and regard them as their elder brothers and leaders.

We must, however, recognize that all educated persons in the community cannot be motivated with such an ideal of service. It must be remembered that man is after all a selfish creature and that in every community there are persons with individualistic trend of mind. There are men amongst us who feel that they can be good *bhagats* of the Gurus without wearing the external symbols of Sikhism. In fact they go further and say that they can follow the true spirit of Gurus' teachings better than those who are obsessed with the external trappings of religion, and they quote the Holy Granth in support of their contention. They feel that symbols which make them obtrusive also expose them to unnecessary attacks and undue attention—they are needlessly made the butt-end of jokes—and their free movements in the modern world are greatly restricted. They even feel that their symbols stand in the way of their worldly progress. Many of my I.M.S. friends have told me so. I know of at least half a dozen, perhaps even more, Sikh I.M.S. officers who have felt it necessary to discard their long hair though they continue to live Sikh lives in other respects and have no faith in any other religion. The number of such men amongst us is increasing at a rapid rate. Must we continue to dub them as apostates and turn them out of our fold? Are we so rich in intellect that we can afford the loss of some of our able men? Can we go on looking with equanimity at the phenomenon which is, I am afraid, spreading and is bound to become even more entrenched as time passes by (as we must be frank enough to recognize that Western learning and modern thought are disruptive of belief in the necessity and efficacy of symbols), and see many of those who acquire knowledge and reputation become in the eyes of the community apostates and outcastes. That is the path to destruction. We must be wise enough to keep men of the type just mentioned within our fold and adjust our ideas—hard as it is bound to be—to the changing conditions. We must enlarge the definition of a Sikh to include such men. Any one who solemnly declares in the presence of God and the Gurus—*Sri Guru Granth Sahib* that he believes in the ten Gurus and their teachings, that besides the Gurus and the *Granth Sahib* he does not recognize any other binding authority in religion, that he belongs to no other religion or community and that he is a Sikh and wishes to be a member of the Sikh fold should be treated as a Sikh and a member of the community.

It is necessary to modify the definition of a Sikh in some such manner as suggested, not only to keep some of our abler men in the fold but also because we owe it to our Gurus to spread their gospel in this country and abroad. And it must be obvious to any thinking man that we cannot expect any success in our propaganda among the educated classes in India or among any people abroad if we stick rigidly to our old standard and symbols. Let us not be slaves to forms and symbols and forget our duty to the Gurus and religion. Let us remember that Guru Nanak came into the world to teach the religion of the spirit and to deliver mankind from the thraldom of *tilak* and *janeu* and *roza*, *tirath* and *haj*, cross and crescent, idols and icons.

The Battle of Life

SARDUL SINGH CAVEESHAR

The ideal man for Guru Gobind Singh was a true soldier, a soldier engaged in battle against ignorance and all that is mean and unrighteous. It was to be the duty of every such soldier to rise higher and higher by sheer force of character, and at the same time help others in such an effort.

So, those who wish to play the part of soldiers must grow strong in body, must grow rich and must become men of strong will. They must overflow with energy of every kind—physical, mental and spiritual. Only in this way can they do their duty well. Social service, philanthropy, patriotism, religion—all these require their support; and the support can only come when the supporters are well endowed with these virtues.

Guru Gobind Singh's emblem for these active virtues was the *kirpan* or sword. Every lion-hearted soldier was required to have this weapon on him which was an outward expression of an inner virtue and to remind him of what his duty was. This sword, or the emblem of the Divine Energy as he called it, was for the reformation of evil and protection of good. Brute force guided by evil hand was to be opposed with all might, but at the same time the less gifted were to be helped and encouraged to prosper by all active and beneficient means.

The second emblem given to his soldiers by Guru Gobind Singh was the comb of purity. Our bodies should be clean and so should be our hearts for only then can a proper use be made of the Divine Energy.

The third virtue necessary for a soldier of Guru Gobind Singh's army was honesty. All dealings between man and man should be based on this virtue, so that no misunderstanding should ever arise. None should misappropriate what belongs to others, because this has been at the root of a greater part of human suffering. It is due to such thievish propensities in man's nature that we find so much of unrest in the world. Guru Gobind Singh put a small hand-cuff on the wrist of every one of his men to let them know that their hands were to be kept back from all such misdeeds.

The other virtue which these soldiers were to possess was chastity;

chastity both in thought and action. Our passions should be like those of an innocent maiden, knowing nothing of evil. No unclean thought should pass our mind, and we should not think evil of any one else. Small trousers (trousers of chastity) were to signify this virtue.

The soldier thus equipped with these arms was ready for the battle of life. Such a soldier is bound to succeed because he is complete in every respect. He becomes a potent force for the upheaval of mankind. But this acquired greatness was not to be used for self-elevation alone; it was to be offered as a sacrifice at the altar of humanity. Each soldier being member of a social group must live as much for himself as for the common brotherhood. It was his duty to sacrifice every attainment of his for the benefit of corporate life because in this alone lay his own greatness and his own salvation. When everyone was imbued with such a spirit of sacrifice, the efforts of each would bring richer fruits for himself and for all else than was possible otherwise. This spirit has its outward manifestation in *kesh* or growing of long hair.

The inner uniform for the soul of a soldier, who has to fight the battle of life, consists of the five virtues—purity, honesty, chastity, power and sacrifice—and their cultivation. The outward uniform is of five symbols—*kangha* (comb), *kara* (wristlet), *kachha* (drawers), *kirpan* (the sword), and *kesh* (long hair). These symbols are expressive of inward virtues and serve as distinguishing marks for those who have taken a vow to serve in the 'order of pure ones' and who have dedicated their lives to the service of God and humanity.

These marks are just as sacred to the Khalsa, the pure ones, as the military uniform is to a soldier, but with this difference that while the other soldiers do not wear uniform all time day, because they are not always 'on duty', a Khalsa is always 'on duty', and must therefore have those virtues ready to help him at all times, for his battle is a never-ending one.

It should be clearly understood that there is nothing esoteric or mystic about the five symbols of the Sikhs. These are what they are, and no extraordinary virtue is claimed for them, except for their ordinary use, as hair for the protection of brain, comb for cleansing the hair, sword for defending the weak, small trousers as a dress adopted for active life and bracelet as a simple ornament. But it is not for any of these uses that the Sikhs wear this uniform. The uniform serves the purpose only of reminding us constantly what army we belong to and what are the 'standing orders' of this army. In our common battles the sight of national flag and the respect for national uniform has often given a firmness and determination to the soldiers who either wavered or were half-hearted: this uniform of the Khalsa also helps to remind them of their duty when they might be in danger of forgetting what they owe to the Order.

It should also be noted that the uniform is like the Royal Insignia of the Royal Dress, proper only for a real king or a real emperor. If a clown were to wear the king's robes, it would not make him a king, rather he would be a disgrace to such a dress. Similarly those who wear the uniform of Guru Gobind Singh's soldiers but do not possess the virtues necessary for fighting the battle of life are a disgrace to the uniform and no more than stage soldiers, worthless for any real purpose.

Importance of Hair and Turban

GANDA SINGH

The *'kes'*, *kesh*, or hair, is an indispensable and perhaps the main symbol of the Sikh faith as enunciated by the tenth Sikh Guru Gobind Singh at the time of the institution of the Sikh baptismal ceremony in 1699. It is an integral part of the human body, created by God and hence calls for its preservation and maintenance as any other part thereof. It was, and still is, therefore, enjoined upon every Sikh at the time of his baptism to preserve the hair of his head, beard and other parts of body uncut, unshorn. With the removal of his hair, a Sikh becomes an apostate and is excommunicated from the Sikh fold. He is then no longer recognized as a Sikh.

This is borne out by the commands of the Guru recorded in his *Hukamnamas* or letters, in the Rules of Sikh Conduct, the *Rahitnamas*, and in other books on the religion and history of the Sikhs compiled and written by contemporary and later writers from the beginning of the eighteenth century to the present day.

The intact preservation of the *kesh* is further emphasized by putting the shaving of hair under taboo as the 'first don't' or *Kurehit* of the Sikh faith. These essentials and don'ts are fundamentals of the Sikh faith and are to be strictly observed as they form an essential part of the Sikh discipline.

The turban of a Sikh is an inseparable part of his dress to keep his hair in good form and properly covered. The turban also adds to the dignity of the person wearing it.

Since the injunction against the shaving of head, beard, etc., is an article, of Sikh faith and is an established historical fact, it should be enough to quote here the relevant pieces from the writings of the Guru, of his close associates and contemporary disciples, and from works on the religion and history of the Sikhs.

Writing to a Sikh congregation on 25 June 1699, Guru Gobind Singh, the tenth and the last Guru of the Sikhs, who initiated the baptismal ceremony among the Sikhs in 1699, said in a letter (*Hukamnama*), 'You should take the Sikh baptism of the Sword, *Khande da Amrit*, from the five (Sikhs), keep (preserve uncut and unshaven) hair, this is our insignia' (*tusan Khande da amrit panjan ton laina, kesh rakhne, ih asadi mohar hai*).

The Guru told his close associate and scribe baptized under the name of Gurbaksh Singh: 'Hair is the insignia of the Guru. He who discards it is an evil spirit, a ghost condemned of the angel of death' (*Mukatnama-Rahitnama*, p.16).

The *Rahitnama* of Prehlad Singh, another associate of the Guru, says that *kesh* should be recognized as an essential part of the Sikh faith (*Rahit-nama*, p.10).

In reply to a question by Nandlal, a contemporary devoted Sikh and author of a number of Sikh treatises, the Guru told him that a Sikh 'should comb' his hair twice a day and wrap his turban properly folded (*Tankhah-nama, Kuliyat*, Bhai Nandlal Goya, p. 180).

According to the *Sri Guru Sobha* of poet Sainapat, who was not only a courtier of Guru Gobind Singh but was also an eyewitness to most of the events of the Guru's life, the Guru issued clear injunctions to his Sikh followers 'not to shave their hair and beard under any circumstances, not even when their parents had died' (as was the practice among the Hindus). 'He who obeyed this injunction as a part of the Sikh discipline, would alone be a true Sikh, the disobedient ones would be ill-circumstanced in the community (vide V, 18-24, 30; VI, 1, etc.).

George Forster, the well-known traveller from East India to England, who passed through the Punjab, the country of the Sikhs, in 1783, wrote from Kashmir to Mr Gregory at Lucknow, on the basis of his personal observations:

They (the Sikhs) permit the growth of the hair of the head and beard, they generally wear an iron bracelet on the left hand, and the use of tobacco is prohibited amongst them. (*Early European Accounts of the Sikhs*, p. 79)

And Major James Browne tells us in his *History of the Origin and Progress of the Sikhs* (1787) that:

From the time, that he (a Sikh) is admitted into the fraternity, he wears a steel ring in one of his wrists, lets hair and beard grow to full length and calls on the name of the Gooroo in confirmation of all engagements. (Introduction, p. xi, ibid, 18)

We shall also give relevant quotations from a few prominent works on the history and religion of the Sikhs, arranged chronologically:

Lt. Col. Malcolm, *Sketch of the Sikhs*, 1812, p. 148:

The disciples of (Guru) Gobind (Singh) were required to allow their hair to grow. . . .

J.D. Cunningham, *A History of the Sikhs*, 1849, pp. 76-8:

They should have one form of initiation, he said, . . . their locks should remain unshorn, they should all name themselves Singhs.

Sir John J.H. Gordon, *The Sikhs*, 1904, pp. 40-1:

In order to mark them as a select body who should be known by outward signs, it was declared that every true Sikh must always have five things with him, their names all commencing with the letter 'K' — namely, Kesh (long hair of the head: The Sikh must never cut his hair or beard). Kangha (comb) to secure the hair tied up in a knot on the top of the head.

M.A. Macauliffe, *The Sikh Religion*, 1909, vol. V, pp. 91-7:

The Guru invited all his Sikhs to attend the great Baisakhi at Anandpur without shaving or cutting their hair. (p. 91)

A supplementary ordinance was now issued that if anyone cut his hair, smoked tobacco, associated with a Mohammedan woman, or ate the flesh of an animal whose throat had been jagged with a knife, he must be rebaptised, pay a fine, and promise not to offend any more; otherwise he must be held to be excommunicated from the Khalsa. (p. 97)

G.C. Narang, *The Transformation of Sikhism*, 1912, pp. 81-2:

This was the significance of the Pahul or the baptism introduced by (Guru) Gobind (Singh). He made it a rule that all Sikhs should wear turbans and always keep the following five kakars or five things whose names begin with 'K', viz, Kesh or long hair and long beard. . . .

Khazan Singh, *History and Philosophy of the Sikh Religion*, 1914, Part 11, p. 544:

The offences subjecting the offender to an immediate excommunication from brotherhood were. . . . (4) tampering with the hair. Such outcastes were held liable to very severe punishment and could be re-admitted only on re-initiation.

C.H. Payne, *A Short History of the Sikhs*, p. 35:

The spirit of brotherhood was still further emphasized by the institution of distinctive dress and the wearing of the five Ks—namely, the Kesh or uncut hair and beard. . . . .

R.E. Parry, *The Sikhs of the Punjab*, 1921, pp. 11-12:

These are the five outward signs of Sikhism, each beginning with the letter 'K', and known as the five Kakar: (1) Kesh or long hair (2) Kangha. . . .

G.B. Scott., *Religion and Short History of the Sikhs*, 1930, pp. 28-9:

Neo-initiates are exhorted. . . Never to cut hair or beard.

Teja Singh, *Essays in Sikhism*, 1944, pp. 32-3:

There was to be no caste among them, and all wear the same signs that is, long hair. . . . They were to call themselves Singhs.

Frederic Pincott, *The Sikh Religion: A symposium* (Pub. 1958), Sikhism, p. 80:

Guru Gobind Singh ordained that every Sikh should always retain on his person five things, each beginning with the letter 'K' that is, Kesh, hair.... A Sikh is to be distinctly different from both Hindu and Muhammadan, both of whom shave the head. A Sikh is never to shave, or even to cut either hair or beard, as long as he lives.

Ranbir Singh, *The Sikh Way of Life*, 1968, p. 102:

The discipline prescribed by the Guru at the time of administering *Amrit* (baptism) is briefly as follows:

A Sikh must wear five Ks.

(1) *Kesh*—Unshorn hair like the ancient sages (rishis) as a pledge of dedication to the Guru. *Kesh* is the first token of Sikh faith. The hair and beard is a part of the personality of the Khalsa.

In addition to these evidences from the writings of the Guru himself and of his close associates and devotees speaking with personal knowledge, and of some eminent scholars, there are the writings of a number of historians and theologians of the eighteenth and nineteenth centuries whose works in Punjabi, Persian and Urdu languages tell us a great deal about the importance attached by the Sikhs to the hair of their head and beard, an essential of their faith. In the first half of the eighteenth century when the Mughal emperors Bahadur Shah (1707-12) and Farrukhsiyar (1713-19), followed by Muhammad Shah (1719-48) and Ahmad Shah (1748-54) had ordered an indiscriminate massacre of the Sikhs wherever found, the Sikhs preferred to lay down their lives than allow their hair to be shaved to save themselves.

So hard were the ordeals through which the Sikhs (also known as Singhs or Khalsa after baptism) had to pass through and so great were the sacrifices that they had to make for their faith—to keep their hair intact to the last breath of their lives—that they are still remembered in the daily Sikh prayer which acts as a source of inspiration to them in difficult times. The relevant passage in the Sikh prayers is as follows:

Think of those Singhs, men and women, who sacrificed their lives at the altar of dharma (duty enjoined by Sikhism), who were cut up joint by joint, who suffered their scalps to be scrapped off, who were broken on the wheels, who were sawn or flayed alive and who abjured not their faith and perjured not their soul but lived their devotion to Sikhism with their hair intact to the last breath of their lives— think of those great martyrs, O Khalsa, and utter Wahiguru, Wahiguru— Wonderful, Wonderful, Wonderful, is the Lord.

All this speaks for itself and should be enough to show conclusively that all Sikhs are required at all times to: (1) keep their hair and beard intact, and (2) to wear turbans as an inseparable part of their dress to keep their hair in proper form.

As Sikhs are easily recognizable by their bearded faces and headgear, *dastar* or turban, they also serve them as helpful deterrents against undesirable acts and behaviour and keep them on the right path. Living among the Hindu and Muslim populations, the Sikhs generally act as neutrals and play the part of reconciling friends when the two happen to fall out on religious and other questions. We have a living example of this. In the 1946 riots at Calcutta, when the whole atmosphere was poisoned with communal virus, the Sikhs played the part of neutrals by helping the sufferers of both sides and bringing about peace and harmony among the blood-thirsty opponents. This was greatly appreciated not only by the people of India but also by the world at large. And historically it stands to the eternal credit of the Sikhs.

The other Sikh essentials, in addition to *kesh* and *kangha* or comb, are *kachha*—a pair of shorts, *kara*—an iron bracelet and *kirpan*—a sword.

The *kangha* speaks for itself. It is to keep the hair well-combed and clean.

The *kachha* reminds a Sikh of his vow to maintain the high standard of sexual morality as ordained by Sikh rules of conduct. It is also an all-time active dress as compared to the *dhoti* or the *salwar*.

Similarly a Sikh's *kara* warns him against un-Sikh like acts and encourages him to be helpful to the deserving needy. Worn on the right hand, as it is, it also provides protection to it when wielding a weapon in fighting.

The *kirpan* of the Sikhs is a weapon of defence against the evil-doers as a last resort. Guru Gobind Singh justified its use as such in his *Zafarnamah* to Emperor Aurangzeb saying:

> *Chun kar az hamah heelte dar-guzashat,*
> *Halal ast burdan ba-shamshir dast.*

That is:

> When all other means have failed to achieve an object,
> it is lawful to take the sword in hand.

These five essential symbols together are called the *Panj Kakar*, or the five Ks.

Turban and Sword of the Sikhs

TRILOCHAN SINGH

niśānī-Sikhī īn pañj harif kāf.
harghiz na bāśad īn pañj muāf.

Know these five K's to be emblems of Sikhism,
Under no condition can one be exempted from them.
Sword and bracelet, drawer and comb—these four,
Without hair the fifth,
all other emblems are meaningless.

Guru Gobind Singh, *Dasam Granth*[1]

Hair of the head is a symbol of faith, intuition
of truth, or the highest qualities of the mind.

G.A. Gaskell, *Dictionary of All Scriptures*

In Sikhism, the human body is sacred because in it shines the brilliant light of wisdom, and more so because it is the home of and dwelling of Spirit of God. It is not flesh and bones that are important, but what makes this flesh and bones appear to be the living image of God on earth, and that is the mind and the spirit of man. The human body becomes meaningful and a dynamic personality with the dazzling light of the mind and the spirit. The two are inseparable from each other. The health of the body depends on the health of the mind and the Spirit.

According to Sikh theology: 'What is in the universe, is also to be found in the human body, and he who seeks it will find it.'[2] 'Such is the divine play of the Creator that He has reflected the whole Cosmos in the human body.'[3] 'In the body, we find the wealth of the whole world.'[4] 'He who is enlightened will search God within himself, and forget all other misleading paths.'[5] This body is the golden fortress in which the eternal Light of His Word shines. It is the temple of God.

In the writings of Guru Nanak, man is represented in his totality; man projected into existence, being-in-spirit and being-in-world. With all the multiplicity around him, man bears within himself the sign and yearning for unity with the Whole. Guru Nanak thus breaks away and stands apart from the Hindu-Buddhist-Jain tradition in this sense, and counsels man against conceiving his transcendence apart from society. Not only does he separate man from humanity but he recognizes that man cannot achieve his transcendence, save through humanity, and he can save his being through communion with God. It is within an enlightened mind and heart that the Cosmos is evaluated and Existence and Being are revealed to man in a mystical communication of its transcendence, 'a communication which man must express in his life and reflect in his actions. It is at the root of the certitude that is responsible for his constant assertion that each man can recognize in every other man the fact of human transcendence.'[6]

surti surati ralāiai etü.
tanü kari tulhā langhih jetü

The Word leads to concentration,
Concentration to knowledge,
This is the riddle of the Guru's Word.
The eternal Light dwells in the human mind.
And the human mind is the emanation of that Light,
And our five senses become the Light's disciple.

Guru Nanak, *Rāga Rāmkalī, Ādi Gurū Granth*, p. 878

The Light reveals itself in the transcendent State or the Tenth Seat of Consciousness (*Dasam Duār*) which is located in the head, and the head is complete and perfect as a seat of revelation only with the hair on it. Without the hair, the head of a mystic is like a maimed limb, never fully capable of containing the full splendour of divine revelation. Mystics like Eckhart and even Plotinus had a glimpse into this transcendent state, just as a mountaineer sees the peak from the foot of the hill. 'Eckhart teaches— at the apex of the mind "there is a Divine Spark" which is closely akin to God, that it is one with Him, and not merely united with Him.'[7]

'Whereas hair on the head, because it grows on the top of the human body, symbolizes spiritual forces and can be equated with the symbolism of water, with the upper ocean, body hair is equivalent to lower ocean.' In general, hair represents energy and is related to the symbolism of levels. That is, hair located on the head stands for higher forces. Hair also signifies fertility. Origen used to say, 'The Nazarites do not cut their hair because all that is done by just men, prospers and their leaves do not fall.' In Hindu symbolism hair like the threads of a fabric symbolizes the lines of force of the universe. A full head of hair represents *elan vital*, and the will to succeed. Hair then comes to symbolize the concept of spiritualized energy. Phaldor, in his *Libro d'oro del Sogno* comments that hair represents the spiritual assets of man. Abundant beautiful hair, for both man and woman, signifies spiritual development. To lose one's hair signifies failure and poverty. Now, the reverse of the loss brought about by forces outside man's control is, in part, willing sacrifice. For this reason Zimmer points out that all 'who renounce and defy the principle of procreation and multiplication of life in order to embark upon the path of total asceticism, are bound on principle to cut their hair short. They must stimulate the sterility of the aged and hairless who form the last link in the chain of generation.'[8]

Zimmer brings out two historical truths. Apostles who believed in a life-affirming view of life, valued and nourished hair on their head, as did the Nazarites. While others who espoused life-denying attitude of life, like the ascetics of various faiths, considered shaving off their hair as the first and foremost duty. Sikhism, as we have already stated, believes in life-affirming view of life.

HAIR IN SEMITIC TRADITION

'Long heavy hair was considered a sign of vitality. In the case of Samson (he having been dedicated to God), the connection of long hair and bodily strength was based on current views. Absolam's famous hair was considered not only an ornament, but as a token of strength. A bald head was an object of mockery.'[9]

'A luxuriant growth of hair on head and chin was regarded by the Hebrews and other Semitic people as an important constituent of manly grace. Solomon's "youthful horsemen" had long hair on their heads (Josh. Ant, viii, vii, 3). It was admired distinction to have bushy curly locks, black as raven. Amongst women long dark tresses were held most captivating and they have always worn long hair. Men dreaded baldness as suggesting a suspicion of leprosy. (Lev. 13:40) The Babylonians wore their hair long, binding their heads with turban.'[10]

'The Nazarites allowed their hair to grow uncut for religious reason. The High Priest and the priests in general, were expressly forbidden to have their heads shaved. The ancient Egyptians had combs and as the Assyrians also were very careful in dressing their hair, it may be due to mere chance that combs are not mentioned in the Old Testament. The

Assyrians wore their hair in several braids reaching down to the nape of their neck. As a sign of mourning the head was shaved.'

'The Law in Judaism regards it in an entirely different light, as it forbids shaving the head on the ground that Israel belongs to Yahweh only (Deut. xiv:i). Originally shaving in times of mourning indicates that the hair was sacrificed to the dead. The Law also regarded as a heathen custom, the shaving of the head in the centre (Jer. ix:26, 23, xix:27), and forbade it as such to Israelites.' (Lev. xix:27).

'The ancient conception, mentioned earlier, that continuously growing hair like the blood is a sign of vitality, sufficiently explains the sacrifice of the hair. The Rabbinical literature in Judaism reveals that the hair was regarded by the Rabbis as being so powerful an augmentation of beauty that married women were recommended to hide it. A man who curled his hair was regarded as a vain man. While Samson was filled with the Holy Spirit, his hair made a noise like the bells, and the sound was heard from Zorah to Eshtath.' In enumerating the wonders of creation God pointed out to Job the wisdom shown even in the making of hair. 'A penalty of one hundred salaim is imposed by the Rabbi for pulling an antagonist's hair, because human hair is associated with thoughts. The number of the hair of the human head is said to be one billion and seven thousand.'[11]

Among the Hebrews, Arabs and other peoples, cutting the flesh was often associated with shaving the head in mourning, or taking part of the hair to lay on the tomb, or on the funeral pyre. Among the Arabs and Hindus, women in mourning shave their head. The habit of tearing the hair in mourning still persists among the Jews and Hindus. It was also a sign of mourning to let the hair fall unattended and dishevelled (Ezek. 24:17, Judith, 10:3).

Possession of a leader's hair in primitive magic was esteemed a potent means of getting and retaining a hold on his person by his followers. The Arabs used to cut off the hair of prisoners before setting them free. Wisdom in the Semitic faiths was always associated with grey hair. Hoary grey hair on the head was the crown of glory, the reward of a life of righteousness. For grey hair to come down on the grave in peace was a token of a life of God's favour. Grey hair laid in men obligations of honourable and chivalrous conduct. Grey hair was an element of glorious appearance (Mac. 15:31), especially that of divine majesty (Dt. 7:8, Rev. 1:14). The hair of Samson was regarded as the seat of strength (Jg. 16:22). The Jews swore by the hair (Mt. 5). One of the most binding oaths in the East now is by the beard.[12]

HAIR IN THE GREEK PHILOSOPHIC TRADITION

The Greeks loved rich waving hair, the youthful gods Bacchus and Apollo were figured with plenteous locks. Enslaved foreigners were forced to shave. It is the Egyptians who loved completely shaving their heads and faces, and they ridiculed long hair of the Asiatics and Greeks. Women never shaved their hair. Offering the hair to the deity was common among the Greeks and Hindus. The idea more or less consciously underlying these practices probably was, that by means of his hair, part of himself, instinct with his life, the devotee formed a stable link or connection with sanctuary and the deity he worshipped. If an important part of life was conceived as residing in the hair, we can see why that of consecrated persons was so cared for. Priests not only allowed their hair to grow but kept them untouched.[13]

Plato called human hair the natural ornament of the head, and the Greeks, says Prof Becker, 'bestowed great pains on the natural ornament of the head, the hair as Plato calls it. They were averse to having it covered in any manner.' Winkelmann remarks that the natives of the South are endowed with greater profusion of hair than the inhabitants of northern lands, and by the Greeks its growth was carefully cherished as it was thought to contribute greatly to render the figure noble and attractive. No less attention was lavished on the beard, which was not looked on as a troublesome encumbrance but as a dignified ornament of maturity and old age. Hence, the whiskers, the moustaches and the beard were allowed to grow. None of these parts were shorn, but of course there were variations in the wear, according to race, abode, condition and individual character. Compare for instance, the busts of Solon and Lycurgus or those of Plato, Antisthenes and Chryasippus. Also see the busts of Demosthenes, Diogenes, Epicurus, Epimenidus, Euripedes, Epicrates, Aeschines, Aeschylus, Sophoclese, Aristophanes and Zeno. 'Pythagoras kept long hair and beard, etc.' Eratosthenes says, 'as Phavorinus quotes him in the eighth book of his *Universal History*, that Pythagoras was the first man who ever practiced boxing in a scientific manner in the forty-eight Olympiad, having his hair long and being clothed in purple. It is recorded of Servius, the sixth king of Rome that his hair emitted sparks on being combed.'[14]

'Monuments as well as the writers tell us that men wore their hair long in the Homeric period, also down to the fifth century. We sometimes find depicted hair of such length and thickness that it seems almost incredible that a man's hair could have been so much developed.'[15] Epictetus argues strongly in favour of wearing long hair. Flavius Domitianus Augustus persecuted the philosophers and ordered them to go to exile. Some of them, in order to conceal their profession of philosophy, shaved their beards. Epictetus would not take off his. And during those days when one of his companions entreated him: 'Come, then, Epictetus shave yourself.' Epictetus replied, 'If I am a philosopher, I answer, I will not shave myself.' 'But' said the other, 'I will take off your head.' 'If that will do you any good, take it off', replied Epictetus.[16]

'Alexander brought into fashion the custom of shaving, but there can be no doubt that it was partially adopted at a much earlier period, though the practice was certainly regarded as contemptible. Chryasippus expressly states that this new custom of shaving was introduced by Alexander. Plutarch asserts that Alexander caused his soldiers to be shaved from the motives of strategic caution. The innovation was stoutly resisted in many States, and was forbidden by special laws which do not seem to have had much effect.'[17]

HAIR AND SHAVING IN HINDU, JAIN AND BUDDHIST TRADITION

Hair has had a positive and negative value and interpretation in Hindu, Buddhist and Jain tradition. To keep hair is to love vital activities of life, to accept social responsibility and to live in a society as part of society. But to shave the hair means renouncing society, renouncing the social ethics of life.

HAIR: THE GLORY OF MAN'S VITAL ENERGY

According to Apastambha's *Aphorisms*, 'He who wishes to be consecrated according to the rites of the Vedas shall wear all his hair in one knot or let him tie the lock on the crown of head in a knot.'[18] The *Satapatha-Brāhmaṇa* says: 'When he has performed the consecration ceremony (*Abhishekaniya*) he does not shave his hair. The reason why he does not shave his hair is this: that the collected essence of the waters, wherewith he is then sprinkled (anointed), is vigour, and it is the hair of the head that it reaches first when he is sprinkled; hence were he to shave his hair, he would cause that glory to fall off from him, he would sweep it away; therefore he does not shave his hair.'[19] 'The clothing of the twice-born (Brāhmin) should be of linen or cotton or also a deer skin, or a cloth entirely dyed with reddish colour. There should also be girdle of *muṅgā* and he should have matted hair.'[20] *Nāradya Dharmaśastra* says that Brāhmins could not be punished by death sentence even for such heinous crimes as man slaughter. 'A Brahmin must not be subject to corporal punishement. For him shaving his head, banishing him from the town, and parading him on an ass shall be his punishment.'[21] Thus shaving the head was equated with capital punishment for the Brāhmins.

Heinrich Zimmer says, Śiva's tresses are long and matted, partly streaming, partly stacked in a kind of pyramid. This is the hair of the mode yogī of gods. Supra-normal life-energy amounting to the power of magic, resides in such wilderness of hair untouched by scissiors. Similary the celebrated strength of Samson, who with naked hands tore asunder the jaws of a lion and shook down the roof of the pagan temple, resided in his uncut hair. Much of the womanly charm, the sensual appeal to the Eternal Feminine, *das wig—eibliche, le charm eternal,* is in the fragrance, the flow and lustre of beautiful hair. On the other hand, anyone renouncing the generative forces of the vegetable-animal realm revolting against the procreative principle of life, sex, earth and nature to enter upon the spiritual path of absolute asceticism has first to be shaved. He must simulate the sterility of an old man whose hair has fallen, and who no longer constitutes a link in the chain of generation. He must coldly sacrifice the foliage of the head.[22]

Even during the early Buddhist period, shaving was the sign of ugliness and contemptible. But, Buddhism made shaving essential for renunciation. The early Pārsīs also considered shaving a sin and crime. The Epistle of *Manūśkihār*, a Pārsī text says, 'And concerning handsomeness and ugliness in themselves, which are only through having taken up an opinion and belief, there is a change even through time and place; for any of the ancients whose head was shaved was as it were ugly, and it was so settled by law, and it was sin worthy of death for them; and then its habits did not direct the customs of the country to shave the head of man.'[23]

Shaving the hair was also a form of punishment for women. 'When a married woman commits adultery, her hair should be shaved, she shall have to lie on a low couch, receive bad clothings, and the removal of all the sweepings shall be assigned to her as her occupation.'[24]

SHAVING THE HEAD: A SYMBOL OF ESCAPE FROM SOCIAL, POLITICAL AND CULTURAL RESPONSIBILITIES

'Full of hindrance is household life, a path defiled by passion, free as the air is the life of him who has renounced all worldly things. How difficult is it for the man who dwells at home to live the higher life in all its fulness, in all its purity, in all its bright perfection. Let me then cut off my hair and beard, let me clothe myself in orange coloured robes, and let me go forth from a household life to a homeless state.'[25]

The Ṣūfī *derveshs*, the Christian monks, the Hindu ascetics, all shave off their heads with this sense of escape from the mundane world to live purely in the spiritual world. The reason as Zimmer points out is, 'to renounce and defy the principle of procreation and multiplication of life in order to embark upon the path of total asceticism', and this principle is inevitably associated with shaving the hair. Heinrich Zimmer adds:

The ascetic hostility to the hair of the human organism is so excessive in the extreme sect of the Jains that they will tolerate no hair whatsoever on the person of an ordained holyman. Part of their ritual of ordination consists in a thorough weeding out of every single hair on the head and the body. Here the idea of the tonsure is, so to say carried to its limit; and correspondingly, the Jaina idea of self-renunciation is drastic beyond bounds. In accordance with their archaic, fundamentalist and thoroughgoing doctrine, the Jains so scheduled their discipline of bodily mortification, that in old age these ideally culminate in death from an absolute fast. As with the hair, so with the last vegetable requirement of the flesh, the revolt against the principles of life is pressed to the end.[26]

THE HAIR, THE COMB AND THE TURBAN OF THE SIKHS

We have already stated earlier in this paper that according to Sikh philosophy of a physically complete man, a human being must preserve all his hair on his head and face as an essential part of his body. Just as the skull performs the protective function of the brain, the hair as an inseparable part of the skull performs the function of the preservation of the *elan vital* of a human being. The complete Man, the Man who is conceived in Sikh scriptures as a man with hair and turban on his head— '*sābat-sūrat dastār sirrā*: Complete Man with hair, beard and turban on his head'.[27]

The hair of the head is also inseparably connected with the comb and turban in Sikh discipline. The continued association of the comb as one of the Ks (*kaṅghā*: comb) signifies that the hair should be kept clean and healthy like other parts of the body. Matted hair or dishevelled hair is not permitted as it is a sign of lethargy, uncleanliness, indifference to social responsibility and cynical attitude to life. Going out bareheaded in the streets is an offence. Not to keep the hair clean by shampooing it regularly is also a serious transgression of the Sikh Code of Conduct.

In the classical Indian tradition, we have already shown that there were two ideals: one of the recluse, who shunned society and preferred the life of cloister or the cave; the other of the *Ṛṣi* or *Kṣatriyā* who lived in society and accepted all responsibilities and challenges of life and yet he was wedded to righteousness and justice:

Dande eva hi rajendra
Ksatradhrama na mundam

Mahabharata, Santi-parva, 23, 46

Commenting on it Dr Radhakrishnan wrote, 'His *Svadharma* or law of action requires him to engage in battle. Protection of right by accepting battle, if necessary, is the social duty of Kṣatriyā and not renunciation. His duty is to maintain order by force and not become an ascetic by shaving off his hair.' 'O thou best of men' says the author of *Mahābhārata* (*Udyoga Parva*), 'there are only two types who can pierce the constellation of the sun and reach the sphere of Brahm. The one is the *sannyāsin* who is steeped in Yoga and the other is the warrior who falls in the battle fighting.'[28] Guru Gobind Singh combined the holiness of the Rishi (*Ṛṣi*) and Christ with the social and political responsibility of the *Kṣatriyā* and gave to the world the Khālsā ideals, which come very near Plato's ideal of Philosopher King; the Philosopher with hair and beard and the highest enlightenment and administrative ability.

The hair of the Khālsā is sacred to him because the Five Beloved Knights (*Pañj Piāre*) of Guru Gobind Singh anointed them with *amrit*; the baptismal water of immortality. The hair, the head, the mind and the consciousness (*surta*) have been made alive and vibrant with a new life.

When He touched my hair and blessed me, how can I bear my hair being shorn. The Sikh is the dedicated. I nestle the fragrance of His touch in my tresses. . . . The inspired personality of this Brotherhood is song-strung, love-strung, gentle, fearless, death despising, even death courting, seeking no reward for incessant self-sacrifice in the name of the Master, dying like moths round the lamp, living like heroes, shining like orbs, intoxicated, sweetly exhilarated every moment of life, elevated above sorry details of things, wishing well to the whole universe of life, and desiring nothing but the lyrical repetition of His Name. . . . The breath of Man is to resound with it, his pores to flow with its nectarian bliss. The eyes go half-upwards under the upper lids, the forehead seems to be filled with nectar. . . . My Brotherhood of the Khalsa is scattered in the history of man in rare persons. All those who call themselves Brothers (Khalsa), but are not so inwardly, spiritually intentionally, consciously and subconsciously of the Guru, are struck off the Roll.[29]

Thus the hair of the Sikh is a symbol of his vow to live for the love of

God; a vow to seek immortality through contemplation and action, a vow to dedicate mind; body and soul at the altar of Truth; Justice Freedom for which the Gurus lived and died. Personal *muktī* (liberation) and life in heaven are never the aim of an enlightened Sikh. The hair must be neatly tied in a tress knot on the apex of the head and a comb tucked in it, ready for use at any time, and a turban tied round it. The turban of the Sikhs is thus an inseparable part of his religious and cultural personality.

All the Sikh Gurus kept hair and beard, and all the Sikh Gurus and Apostles wore turbans. The oldest painting of Guru Nanak, which Ram Rai took with him from his father Guru Har Rai, now preserved at Dehradun as a relic, shows Guru Nanak wearing the *Paṭhan* type turban, which was worn by the Punjabis. This type of turban with little modification continued to be worn by the first five Gurus. It was a little smaller in size, and worn more gracefully than the common Pathan did, in the manner of the Sufi saints. From the time of Guru Hargobind the Rajput style became common, and it was patronized even by the Mughal rulers. Out of this style the Sikh warriors who carried a quoit on their heads, developed variations which we see in the paintings of the Sikh warriors. The Sikh princes of Ranjit Singh's durbar developed a distinct style of their own, out of which emerged many modern styles, fundamentally resembling one another.

NOTES

1.   *nišānī Sikhī īn panj harif kāf.*
      harghiz na bāśad īn panj muāf.
      karā kārdo, kachh, kanghā, bidān.
      bila kesh hech ast, jumlā nishān.
      Guru Gobind Singh, *Sarb Loh Granth* (*MS: Hazur Sahib*), *Dasam Granth* (*Sangrur MS*).
2.   *Adi Guru Granth*, Guru Nanak, *Maru*, p. 110, see also, p. 698.
3.   Ibid., Guru Amar Das, *Rag Majh*, p. 117.
4.   Ibid., *Rag Suhī*, p. 754.
5.   Ibid., *Rag Suhī*, p. 762.
6.   Trilochan Singh, *Guru Nanak's Religion: A Comparative Study of Religions*, p. 15.
7.   W.R. Inge, *Christian Mysticism*, p. 115.
8.   J.E. Cirlot, *Dictionary of Symbols*, p. 134.
9.   *Jewish Encyclopaedia*, New York, 1925.
10.   James Hastings, *Dictionary of the Bible*.
11.   *Jewish Encyclopaedia*, New York, 1925.
12.   James Hastings, *Dcitionary of the Bible*.
13.   Ibid.
14.   Dharam Anant Singh, *Plato and the True Enlightener of the Soul*, pp. 156-7.

15. Blummer, *The Home Life of the Ancient Greeks*, p. 64.
16. *Discourses of Epictetus*, tr. G. Long Bk. I, Chap. 11.
17. Dharam Anant Singh, *Plato and the True Enlightener of the Soul*, p. 159.
18. *Apastamba's Aphorisms*, tr. George Buhler, p. 8.
19. *The Satpatha Brhmana* (Mahayana School), tr. Julius Eggeling, p. 120.
20. *Anugita*, tr. Kashinath Trinibak Tilang, p. 361.
21. *Nrada Dharamaśāstra*, tr. Julius Jolly, p. 163.
22. Heinrich Zimmer, *Myths and Symbols in Indian Art and Civilization*, p. 157.
23. *Epistles of Manuskihr*, p. 408.
24. *Narada Dharmaśāstra*, p. 83.
25. *Tevigga Suttanta*, tr. T.W. Rhys David, p. 187.
26. Heinrich Zimmer, *Myths and Symbols in Indian Art and Civilization*, p. 166.
27. This hymns of Guru Arjan in *Rag Maru, Sohile* (*Adi Guru Granth*, p. 1084), which is a treatise of Muslim ceremony of circumcision, also gives a glimpse of the philosophy of the Sikh Gurus. The man who is conceived to be physically and spiritually the image of God, is conceived in Sikh theology a complete man as conceived by God with hair and turban on his head.
28. Dr S. Radhakrishnan, *Gīta*, tr., p. 112.
29. Puran Singh, *The Spirit Born People*, pp. 122-4.

The Sikh Symbols

BHAGAT SINGH

Ever since the dawn of religious consciousness in man, 'symbolism' has, in one form or another, played a significant role in religion. Realising the inability of common people to grasp or retain the import of abstract principles of concepts, the wise men gave some kind of concrete shape to the ideas, in the form of symbols, for their appeal to imagination, sentiments or beliefs in religion.

There can be no doubt that *kesh*, unshorn locks or long hair and beard, constitute the Sikh's chief symbol. Parting with the *kesh* for a Sikh constitutes apostasy. That the nine predecessors-in-office of Guru Gobind Singh grew long hair and beard, is not open to any doubt. However, they did not wear long hair as a matter of compulsion, but perhaps, just like other saints and ascetics, because of the belief that submission to God's will was an article of their creed; no one can claim to abide by God's will, if he resorts to the removal of this gift of nature.

THE INDIAN TRADITION

In making the *kesh* an insignia of the Khalsa, what exactly weighed with the tenth Guru is not fully known. Presumably he wanted to invest his disciples with an insignia that would proclaim their identity and this was amply justified by the long series of martyrdoms which adorn the pages of the Sikh history and show that as a symbol, the *kesh* were held dearer than life itself. Even till this day, our prayer contains a significant wish—'that the disciple's faith may be preserved with the *kesh* unto the last breath'. There would appear to be other sound reasons also for this symbol.

Speaking in the context of tradition, it is to be observed that the Gurus, like *rishis* of old and founders of other great religions of the world, wore long hair. In ancient India there was a time when in Hindu society the removal of long hair was regarded as a penalty equivalent to capital punishment. According to the Hindu tradition, the growing of long hair was a well-recognized symbol of dedication, and still continues to be so among several sects of the Hindu ascetics throughout India. The Khalsa, created by the tenth Master for the service to mankind was nothing if not complete dedication to a continual fight against tyranny and oppression anywhere, in any form or shape.

BIOLOGICAL SIGNIFICANCE

Unfortunately the biological significance of *kesh* has not been fully investigated or understood. That there is some mysterious relation between hair and physical virility is borne out by the well-known story of Samson and Delilah in the Old Testamant. Some may raise questions on the paring of nails too since they are nature's growth. The portion of the nails intended to be pared is physiologically dead, as indicated by the line of demarcation. For a similar reason, the dead hair is to be combed out every day and not retained and matted.

SECULAR REASON

A Sikh is enjoined to lead a house-holder's life, and not the life of a monk or sanyasi. The practice of cutting the hair of the head or clean shaving of the head and the facial hair, or pulling them off one by one, like the Jain monks, and the religious observance of tonsure, practised in the Roman Catholic and Orthodox Eastern Churches, are signs of renunciation of worldly life.

It is well understood that every member of the Khalsa is expected to be soldier-saint, a saint primarily and a soldier secondarily. If wearing of long hair had not, in some way or to some extent, been conducive to spiritual development, great men even of the twentieth century like Maharishi Rabindranath Tagore, Aurobindo Ghosh and the Russian count, Tolstoy, and many others would not have been so particular in the matter of keeping long hair and flowing beard—both manifestations of their inner spiritual sublimity.

AESTHETIC

Standards of beauty, in the case of male as well as female, have never been uniform, in all climes and in all ages. But the primary standard is the one which the Creator, in His Divine wisdom, has set for mankind. The examples in the case of animals, a cock's comb, a lion's mane, etc., are too many and obvious to need even a passing reference. And shall we have the audacity to say that God erred in the case of human male and was right in the case of other animals?

MARTIAL

For the forces of militant Khalsa, which the tenth Guru raised to liberate the mother-land, it was evidently necessary to prescribe some kind of uniform. And what better uniform could be prescribed than the *kesh*—at once natural, dignified, protective and sometimes time-saving.

· And it is needless to emphasize the value of uniform. We all know that a soldier, without uniform, however smart, strong, courageous and deft in the use of arms, has no place in any army. The Britishers easily recognized the value of the Sikh symbols as an art of military discipline, and insisted upon the Sikh recruits being Keshdharis.

Mr Duncan Greenless, a renowned scholar of Comparative Religion and author of The World Gospel Series, considers *kesh* as a test of the disciple's courage and firmness, for 'It costs something to proclaim oneself a Sikh, thus visibly, when Sikhs were hunted down for torture and death. Thus, wearing of long hair trained men in courage, in being ready at all times, to be martyrs for the faith.' Similar opinion, is expressed by Professor Om Parkash Kahol who states that: 'No man could be a Sikh secretly and the community relied only on the integrity of those men of steel who abided by the discipline of their Guru.'

SOCIAL AND ORGANIZATIONAL

The social reason for the *kesh* may be that this symbol promotes 'group-consciousness', and fosters feelings of brotherhood, strengthens *espirit de corps*, binds each individual to be morally worthy of the whole, creates a healthy pride and a sense of participation in all the work of brothers of the same society.

This has been, however, a mere academic discussion against the background of history. Devout Sikhs have never questioned the rationale of long hair (or any other symbol), but grow it simply to obey the behest of the Guru, and regard it as a sacred gift. They endeavour, at least, to look not only like him but also like one another. It is well known that this symbol has been hallowed by the blood of a long line of martyrs, and to discard it, is to wipe out the most glorious chapter of the Sikh history and traditions. For these reasons it is loved by an overwhelming majority of Singhs, and anyone parting with it is still looked down upon as a renegade.

Unless, therefore, the Khalsa wants to perish, the importance of the *kesh*, should be emphasized, for it is this symbol which has established the community and perpetuated its existence. These signs of the faith were given by the Guru, and in the words of Duncan Greenlees, 'a Sikh who gives them up will be despised as a coward and a traitor to the deeds and ideals of his fathers, but he who clings to them even at the cost of the laughter of the ignorant, will earn the respect of his neighbours, and bring added glory to the Guru and to all those who died for the truth in former days'.

Mrs P.M. Wylam, the well-known Sikh-English lady, regards these symbols as a common denominator binding the Sikhs, and is of the view that when a Sikh discards his hair he becomes rootless and much of his spiritual strength is lost.

Another English admirer of Sikhism, Miss Jeanne Culler, addressing a gathering of Sikh youth, writes:

Eliminate your symbols, my Sikhlings, and watch the Khalsa crumble. Take off the turban, shave the beard, cut the hair or throw aside the *Kada*, I can tell you truthfully, the result would be embarrassing as well as disastrous. These five symbols have held the Sikhs in united brotherhood. They serve to make a Sikh feel and act as a Sikh. They endow him with a courage to accomplish feats, which otherwise would be impossible for an average man. To make a long story short, the five symbols have a psychological bearing on the man who wears them. They are a manifestation of the Guru Eternal.

SYMBOLS WITHOUT CHARACTER

Horace Ship, in his illuminating book *Faiths that Moved the World* is of the view that form, or symbol, while it gives strength of unity and authority of tradition, building together, what might otherwise fall apart, has one fault which inevitably threatens any kind of ritual: it can easily become a dead letter, from which the spirit has departed. That was the reason why the Sikhs who merely wore the outward insignia of the faith but did not live the life prescribed, were declared by the Guru, to be stupid impostors. How humorously but pointedly, the great Guru, brought home to the Sikhs the importance of the spirit behind the symbols by citing the example of clothing a donkey in the skin of a lion, so that the beast remained an object of terror until the truth came to light as a result of his braying.

Truly speaking, any symbol, however sacred, is not an end in itself, but only a means to a higher and nobler end. If this is fully understood, not only will the Sikh uniform be honoured but its wearers themselves will be worshipped, as were the Singhs of yore. The present day Singhs must, therefore, so conduct themselves that everyone of them should be looked upon as a member of Civic Guard as intended by the Guru. In that capacity, each will be serving not only his community but also the country, nay the entire humanity, and in the process will further the cause of true religion. This is by no means easy. The moral and spiritual regeneration of a vast and scattered community is a gigantic task. But the more difficult the task, the more serious and sustained is the effort that we shall have to make.

THE COMB

The symbol directly connected with the *kesh*, is the *kangha*, or the comb. It is a necessary adjunct of unshorn hair. In order to promote cleanliness and health, the hair is not to be matted as by ascetics. The comb keeps the hair securely underneath the turban. So particular was the Guru about the use of a comb that every Singh was enjoined not merely to keep it, but also to use it daily. Its ethical value lies in its being an emblem of purity and self-examination which symbolizes discipline of mind. While combing the hair physically, we can always utilize the psychological principle of auto-suggestion, and improve ourselves morally and spiritually.

THE BANGLE

The *kara*, or the bangle, must invariably be made of steel, and not of any other metal, such as gold (the gold *kara* came into vogue among the rich). Its physical utility is not quite apparent; but to my surprise, an old, well-educated Hindu gentleman, was found wearing this *kara* as a cure for acidity of the blood.

Ethically, the *kara* symbolizes a determination to be honest in dealings, as it is a sort of handcuff or restraint placed by the divine Master, in respect of deeds, which may pollute the hands of Sikhs and bring discredit to the community as well as to the Guru. This bangle acts also as a warning, which, if ignored, may at some time or the other, invite the Law's handcuffs. In that way, it can serve as an aid in shaping a Sikh's character. As an unbroken circle, it also symbolizes the continuity of existence and timelessness. Incidentally, a *kara* is worn by all the Sahajdhari Sikhs as a matter of identity. As in olden days, so, even today, in Bengal particularly, a girl on marriage wears an iron bangle as a mark of *sohag* (pride of belonging to her beloved husband). The *kara* worn by a Sikh reminds him similarly of his ties to his Guru—ties of obedience, devotion and love for the divine Master.

THE SHORTS

The fourth symbol is the *kaccha* or shorts. The antiquity of this garment goes beyond the time of Sri Ram; and it is recorded that, pleased with the signal and devoted service rendered by Hanuman, Sri Ram bestowed a *kaccha* upon the devotee.

The physical utility of the shorts has been universally recognized and, in its various forms, has been adopted. Otherwise too it is a simple, cheap, easy to make, and easy-to-wear, garment highly useful for brisk movement. It must always be worn for perpetual readiness.

Ethically, the *kaccha* promotes chastity, equally essential for members of the order. It was this symbol to which our saviour Guru Gobind Singh invited the attention of Bhai Joga Singh, when the latter was rescued from the clutches of a harlot. As an utility-working garment, the *kaccha* is worn by girls and women while working in cooperative settlements in Israel and Soviet Union. It allows easy movement, comfort in work and serves as a protective garment.

THE *KIRPAN*

The *kirpan*, or sword, the fifth and last symbol, is primarily for self-defence. Its utility, on that ground in those days was too obvious in order to determine which of these two elements is predominant in a particular case.

That the precise physical state of the hair is always relevant to its symbolic meaning, but is never itself the deciding factor, can be made clear from the example of the Chinese pigtail, which superficially resembles the Hindu *shikha* (scalp-lock) in appearance. The Manchus, a foreign dynasty, in fact first instituted the pigtail among the Chinese in AD 1644 as a sign of their subjection. It later became accepted as a characteristic Mandarin custom, even as a sign of honour. In the mid-nineteenth century, the Taiping rebellion and in the early twentieth century Sun Yat-sen's movement and others sought to dispose of the pigtail, remembering its original significance. The Taipings did so by wearing long the entire hair of their heads and so became known as the 'long-haired rebels', whereas the twentieth-century revolutionaries proceeded to cut all their hair short, literally throwing the pigtail away. The complete contrast between these two outcomes of a single impulse is not without interest for our study.

In Sikhism, the injunction to remain unshorn is expressly associated with the ceremony of initiation, and it is in that context that we must primarily explain it. Now every initiation rite evidently possesses the nature of an investiture or conferment, since through it some new status with its consequent rights and obligations is conferred symbolically upon the neophyte, and he or she enters on a new mode of existence. But every initiation rite necessarily also contains a somewhat less obvious element of renunciation or divestiture, whereby the neophyte symbolically discards or has taken away from him attributes of his old status and mode of existence. One must ritually first abandon the previous course or phase of social existence in order to properly enter the new. Admittedly, the positive element of investiture or conferment generally predominates in initiation rites, but the element of renunciation or divestiture is always present to some degree. This negative element may even be uppermost in certain cases, for example, in initiation into monkhood.

I want now to draw attention to a class of initiation rites of this latter kind that were widely prevalent in the Punjab at the time in question, and its possession and use made the Sikhs what they are. It is insignia of the temporal power, a symbol of sovereignty, of dignity, an emblem of divine energy.

The very possession of a *kirpan* fills its wearer with courage and confidence even though he may have no occasion to use the weapon, just as a pocket filled with money has a psychological effect, in contrast with an empty one. Doubts have been expressed in certain quarters about the cult of the *kirpan* and its utility as a weapon in modern times when so much stress is being laid on the attainment of peace through the practice of non-violence. It may be said in reply that the *kirpan* is a weapon of defence, not of offence, and it is to be used not on any simple provocation, but only as the last resort. It is handier and safer than firearms, which, though more effective are more dangerous to keep. In India, the question of licence apart, a *kirpan* of a convenient size is much easier to keep and safer to use.

It will be observed that of the five, the two, namely *kara*, and *kirpan* must be of steel which in itself is a symbol of strength—a functional and not an ornamental metal.

As a result of the demoralizing policy of the British, the *kirpan* of the usual size was replaced by a miniaturized version, attached to or embedded in the comb. And it was not without a prolonged struggle that the restrictions imposed on this right, as also on the length of the *kirpan*, were withdrawn. But after independence when the Constitution of India, as a Sovereign Independent Republic was drawn up it became an easy matter. In explanation I to Article 25 (1) of the Constitution, which conferred upon every citizen the freedom of conscience, of profession and practice and propagation of his religion, it was laid down that the wearing and the carrying of the *kirpan* shall be included in the profession of the Sikh religion.

It is, however, regretted that the number of Sikhs who wear a *kirpan* of the usual size, is still very small. The *kirpan* could be made of a suitable decorative size, attractive enough to be worn as a part of the normal attire.

The symbols thus, have, not only an utilitarian but also organizational, ethical and spiritual values, which need to be realized and nursed and so must be worn both outwardly and inwardly.

The Five Symbols of Sikhism

J.P.S. UBEROI

THE STRUCTURAL METHOD

The custom of wearing long and unshorn hair (*kesh*) is among the most cherished and distinctive signs of an individual's membership of the Sikh Panth, and it seems always to have been so. The explicit injunction to this effect was established early as one of the four major taboos (*Kurehit*) that are impressed upon the neophyte at the ceremony of initiation into Sikhism, and unshorn hair is one of the five symbols that every Sikh should wear on his person. Yet there exists hardly any systematic attempt in Sikh studies to explain and interpret the origin and significance of this custom.[1] As a religious system, Sikhism is antiritualistic in its doctrine, content and general tone, so that a study of the few obligatory rites and ceremonies that are associated with it in its institutional or social aspect should be of considerale interest for its own sake. Moreover, if our investigation of the connection between the nature of Sikhism as a whole and its five symbols, including the specific custom of remaining unshorn, were to be made in a comparative and empirical spirit and according to rules of method capable of universal application, we may expect that the solution of this particular problem would also elucidate certain general problems of the sociology of religion, for example, regarding the nature of religious innovation and its institutionalization.

I am not myself able to adequately investigate the problem at present, since I do not possess the requisite linguistic proficiency to study the original Punjabi sources, and without acquiring a first-hand knowledge of them, I cannot proceed satisfactorily. The argument and interpretation presented in this paper will be based solely on the information available in English, and for my reliance on second-hand sources that are incomplete and liable to error. I offer an apology in advance. I shall hope, nevertheless, that the sociological method or scheme of interpretation that I shall adopt might invoke some interest. For the results achieved, or those capable of being achieved, in a line of enquiry depend not only on the evidence examined and its authenticity, but also on the method of analysis and interpretation followed.

The particular method adopted here, which may be called the structural method, implies that, for a proper theoretical understanding or explanation, the ceremonial custom or rite in question must be viewed from two inter-related aspects. We should attempt to determine (1) its ideological meaning within a particular system of symbolic thought, and (2) its social function within a particular social system of groups and categories. The first aspect, which we may call explanation at the level of culturally conditioned thought and belief, is a matter of examining the ceremony or rite as a condensed statement, the symbolic expression of certain characteristic cultural ideas and values. In the second aspect of my study I move to the level of institutionalized behaviour or social action, and seek to relate the rite and the social occasion of its performance to the wider social system of the group or category of persons who recognize the obligation to perform it. In neither case do we consider the particular rite in isolation but bear in mind the context of the other rites with which it is associated in reality, and at either level of analysis our understanding proceeds by seeking to relate the part of its larger whole, the piece to the pattern. Only after these necessary steps have been taken in the context of a particular culture or society, may we rightly proceed further to compare the meanings and social functions of similar rites observed in two or more different cultures, or even of the same rite in a single culture during dif-ferent historical periods.

Combining these two aspects or levels of thought and behaviour which it is convenient to distinguish for analysis, we may state the central assumption of our procedure in the form that all ceremonies and rites are expressive and affirmative in character, that is, they embody and communicate abstract meanings and values in concrete shape. The obligatory and oft-repeated social performance of a body of rites serves to give definitive expression and form to a people's collective life and ideas. It affirms to themselves and to others the structural coherence of their particular pattern of culture, thought and social organization as an ordered whole, and contributes to maintain and develop that pattern from generation to generation. These effects together constitute, according to our main theoretical assumption, the *raison d'être* of ritual behaviour and symbolic thought.

It will be apparent to anyone who has made the attempt that an investigation of the exact meaning and social function of a rite is a complex and difficult task. It is a process like that of ascertaining the grammar and syntax of a language, its structure as against its lexicon, which cannot be done by a simple enquiry from a native speaker or informant. For a ritual is capable by its inner nature of involving several abstract meanings and social references and, moreover, these generally are not readily accessible at the conscious surface of life but require to be extracted, as it were, from the subconscious. It is, therefore, especially necessary in this field of study to avoid all easy inferences from intuition or deductive reasoning and to adhere to explicitly formulated rules of method.

SYMBOLS, SECTS AND INITIATIONS

The cultural association of a man's hair, especially long hair, with magical or sacred ideas is known from many parts of the world. It is well recognized in general terms to be a symbol of manliness, virility, honour, power, aggression and so on. For example, in very early Europe, the Achaeans, who conquered Greece, customarily wore their hair long and wild. The Semitic story of Samson and Delilah, as told in the Old Testament, well illustrates the virtue of remaining unshorn. We can readily locate many similar examples in classical Hinduism. The Institutes of Manu specify: 'Even should a man be in wrath, let him never seize another by the hair. When a Brahman commits an offence for which the members of other castes are liable to death, let his hair be shaved off as sufficient punishment.'

We should, however, be careful to remember that, like all sacred or tabooed objects, long hair can also equally carry the opposite connotation; it can be regarded, especially when unkempt, as signifying something unclean, dangerous or abandoned. We must thus refer, according to the rules of our method, to the actual context and situation in order to determine which of these two elements is predominant in a particular case.

I now wish to discuss some of the initiation rites. These were the rites of renunciation (sanyasa) through which an individual obtained entrance to one or other of the medieval mendicant orders (sanyasis), etc. It is my contention that an examination of this class of rites with the details of the Sikh initiation rite, borne in mind, shows a remarkable relation of structural inversion to exist between the two. I want to suggest that, in terms of the symbolic language and ritual idioms of the times, at least one cultural meaning of the Sikh initiation rite was that it stood as the antithesis of the rites of Hindu renunciation.

A sanyasi is a person who, having passed through the first three stages (*ashramas*) of Brahmanical Hinduism, renounces the world and is cared for by others. It may perhaps be that the sanyasi religious orders were older than the Brahmanical institution of sanyasa, the fourth and last stage of life. At any rate, the orders seem to have been open to entry by the individual person of almost any physical age. The sanyasi orders had decayed significantly during the Buddhist period and then split into sub-orders with heterodox creeds. They were reformed by Sankaracharya, whose four disciples instituted four *maths* (orders) that later developed into numerous *padas* (sub-orders). Each sub-order was said to have two sections, one celibate and mendicant, and the other not. All sanyasis were further graded according to four degrees of increasing sanctity (*Kavichar, Bahudhak, Hans* and *Param Hans*).

The sanyasi initiation rite was and continues to be essentially as follows.[2] The candidate intending to attain renunciation first goes on a pilgrimage to find a guru, who should be a Brahman, and the latter satisfies the former regarding his fitness, and proceeds to initiate him. The neophyte commences with the *shradha* (obsequies) to his ancestors to fulfil his obligations to them. He next performs the sacrificial *baji hawan* and gives away whatever he possesses, severing all connection with the world. His beard, moustache and head are entirely shaved (*mundan*), retaining only the scalp-lock (*shikha*), and the sacred thread is put aside. He then performs the *atma-shraddha* or his own death rites. (An initiated sanyasi is thus counted as socially deceased, and when he dies is not cremated but buried in a sitting posture without ceremony.) The scalp-lock is now cut off, and the neophyte enters the river or any other body of water with it, and the sacred thread in hand, and throws both away, resolving 'I am no one's and no one is mine.' On emerging from the water he starts naked to the north but the guru stops him and gives him a loin-cloth (*kopin*), staff (*danda*) and a water-vessel (*jalpatra*) kept out of the neophyte's personal property. Finally, the guru gives him the *mantra* (spiritual formula) in secret and admits him to a particular *math* (order), *sampradaya*, etc.[3]

The initiation rite of the jogi order, which was also widespread in the medieval Punjab, is a very similar thing. According to the Punjab Census Reports, 1912, a jogi is a corruption of yogi, a term applied originally to sanyasis well advanced in the practice of *yogabhyasa*.

The Jogis are really a branch of Sannyasis, the order having been founded by Guru Machhandar (Matsyendra) Nath and Gorakh Nath Sannyasis, who were devoted to the practice of yoga and possessed great supernatural power. The followers of Guru Gorakh Nath are absorbed more in the yoga practices than in the study of the Vedas and other religious literature, but between a real good Jogi and a Yogi Sannyasi there is not much difference, except perhaps that the frmer wears the *mudra* (rings) in the ears. The Jogis worship Bhairon, the most fearful form of Shiva.[4]

Their main sub-divisions are stated to be the *Darshani* or *Kanphata* (split-ear), known as Naths, who wear the *mudras* (earrings); and the *Aughar*, who do not.

In jogi initiation, the neophyte (*chela*) is first made to fast for two or three days. A knife is then driven into the earth,[5] and the candidate vows by it not to (1) engage in trade, (2) take employment, (3) keep dangerous weapons, (4) become angry when abused, and (5) marry. He must also scrupulously protect his ears, for 'a jogi whose ears were cut used to be buried alive, but is now only excommunicated'. The neophyte's scalp-lock is removed by the guru, and he is shaved by a barber; his sacred thread is also removed. He bathes and is smeared with ashes, then given ochre clothes to wear, including the *kafni* (shroud). The Guru-mantra is communicated secretly, and the candidate is now a probationer (*aughar*). After several months of probation his ears are pierced and earrings inserted by either the guru or someone who is adept at it and who is entitled to an offering of a rupee and a quarter. 'The *chela*, hitherto an aughar, now becomes a *nath*, certain set phrases (not mantras) being recited.'[6]

After the initiation, a jogi may either remain a celebate and ascetic mendicant (*Nanga, Naga, Nadi, Nihang,* or *Kanphata*) living on alms; or he may relapse and become a secular jogi (called *Bindi-Nagi, Sanyogi, Gharbari* or *Grihasti*, having property and spouse).

A jogi usually joins one or the other of the various panths or 'doors' (sub-orders), whose traditional number was twelve.

I mention finally the initiation rites of the Dadupanthi order, stated to have been founded by Dadu, a Gaur Brahman, who died in AD 1703.[7] In this rite the guru in the presence of all the sadhus shaves off the neophyte's scalp-lock and covers his head with a skull-cap (*kapali*) like the one which Dadu wore. He dons ochre clothes and is taught the Guru-mantra, 'which he must not reveal'.[8] The rite concludes with the distribution of sweets.

THE SIKH INITIATION AND ITS FIVE SYMBOLS

In my view, there can be little doubt that the taboo against cutting or trimming hair (*Kurehit*) of the Sikh initiation rite is to be understood as a specific inversion in symbolic terms of the custom of total depilation enjoined upon the jogi or sanyasi initiate. The element of symbolic inversion, as I see, is, in fact, much more pervasive, but it has been entirely overlooked owing to the prevalence, among students of religion, of the scholarly method of endlessly adducing parallels and similarities to the neglect of significant relations of contrast, counterpoint, inversion and opposition.[9] In contradistinction to the jogi and sanyasi ritual of nakedness or smearing oneself with ashes, the Sikh neophyte is made to come tidily clothed to the ceremony. The earrings worn by the jogis are specifically forbidden to him.[10] Instead of requiring the sanyasi's resolve. 'I am no one's and no one is mine,' the Sikh rite, emphasizing a new birth, requires the neophyte to affirm that his father is Guru Gobind Singh and his mother is Mata Sahib Kaur, and that he was born in Kesgarh and lives in Anandpur. Even more significantly the initiator, instead of being the individual guru, is a collective group, the Five Loved Ones (*Panj Piare*) composed of any five baptised Sikhs. Instead of Guru-mantra being communicated secretly to the neophyte, as with the sanyasis, jogis and Dadupanthis, the Sikh Gurus' word must be spoken loud and clear by the initiators. Finally, in contrast to the jogi vow never to touch weapons, the Sikh neophyte is invested ritually with the *kirpan* (sword) as one of the five Ks that he must always wear thereafter.

I think we may safely say that the Sikh initiation rite contains a marked theme of inversion in relation to the rites of social renunciation established by the medieval mendicant orders that proceeded Sikhism. Like them, Sikhism was instituted as a religious brotherhood open to all who sought salvation, but its spiritual and social aims were in direct contrast to what theirs had been. Whereas they had sought to obtain emancipation or deliverance through individual renunciation at the price, as their rites signify, of social death, the Sikh community was to affirm the normal social world as itself the battleground of freedom. That is why, in my opinion, its initiation rite makes the positive theme of investiture prevail wholly over the negative theme of divestiture, and taking certain widely established customs of renunciation, emphatically inverts them. The meaning of being unshorn, in particular, is thus constituted by the 'negation of the negation'. It signifies the permanent renunciation of renunciation.

This hypothesis, however, is not complete; it requires a further consideration regarding the five Ks. We have so far concentrated our attention on the initiation rite itself and attempted to understand the meaning of *kesh* in that context, but the five symbols of Sikhism are worn for life. Now, following the initiation, the sanyasi custom is either to wear all their hair or shave it all. The Jatadhari jogis follow the former course— though among all jogis the significant of renunciation seems to be borne primarily by their pierced ears and earrings. The important order of Bairagis also keeps long hair,[11] whereas the Uttradi Dadupanthis shave their head, beard and moustache.[12] The Rasul Shahis, a Muslim order founded in the eighteenth century, also shave completely the head, moustache and eyebrows.[13] In all instances, where long hair is worn, it is worn as matted hair (*jata*), frequently dressed in ashes. According to the Sikh custom, on the other hand, unshorn hair (*kesh*) is invariably associated with the comb (*kangha*, the second of the five Ks) which performs the function of constraining the hair and imparting an orderly arrangement to it. This meaning is made even clear by the custom of the Sikh turban. The *kesh* and *kangha* thus form an unitary pair of symbols, each evoking the meaning of the other, and their mutual association explains the full meaning of *kesh* distinct from *jata*. The *jata*, like the shaven head and pierced ears, symbolizes the renunciation of social citizenship; *kesh* and *kangha* symbolize its orderly assumption.

The *kirpan* (sword) and the *kara* (steel bracelet) similarly constitute another pair of symbols, neither of which can be properly understood in isolation. Without going into the evidence, I merely state that in my view the steel bracelet imparts the same orderly control over the sword which the comb does over the hair. The *kirpan*, in its conjoint meaning with the *kara*, is a sword ritually constrained and, thus, made into the mark of every citizen's honour, not only of the soldier's vocation. Finally, the *kachha*, a garment for the loin and thighs, the last of the five Ks, is also to be understood as an agent of constraint like the comb and the bracelet, though the subject of its control is not overly stated. Obviously, it is a sartorial symbol signifying manly reserve in commitment to the procreative world as against renouncing it altogether.

In case it might be objected to that I am merely profaning the mystery in advancing the last hypothesis, I hasten to quote Guru Gobind Singh himself on the subject:

Ajmer Chand inquired what the marks of the Guru's Sikhs were, that is, how they could be recognized. The Guru replied, 'My Sikhs shall be in their natural form, that is without the loss of their hair or foreskin, in opposition to ordinances of the Hindus and the Muhammadans.'[14]

We can now formulate the proposition that the primary meaning of the five symbols, when they are taken together, lies in the ritual conjunction of two opposed forces or aspects. The unshorn hair, the sword and the implicit uncircumcised male organ express the first aspect. They are assertive of forceful human potentialities that are by themselves amoral, even dangerous, powers. The combination of the two aspects is elaborated in the form of three pairs of polar opposites (*kangha/kesh: kara/kirpan: kachha/*uncircumcised member), thus generating, with one term left unstated, the five Sikh symbols. The aspect of assertion and the aspect of constraint combine to produce what we may call, for want of a better word, the spirit of affirmation, characteristic of Sikhism.

HINDUISM AND SIKHISM

So much then for the structure of cultural meanings. We must now turn, although very briefly and simply, to the second level of analysis required by our method, and consider the wider social context of Sikhism's origin and growth. I do not here give all the evidence or make every qualification, but state the problem in broad and general terms as follows:

The Hindu system of social relations called caste, using that term to include *varna* as well as *jati*, is, in fact, only the half of Hinduism. The whole Hindu *dharma* is described by the term *varnasramadharma*, that is, caste as well as the institution of the four stages or statuses (*ashramas*) of individual life. If sociologists have hitherto concentrated on the institution of caste to the exclusion of the latter institution, I cannot claim to understand their reasons. For the social system of caste was always surrounded in reality by a penumbral region, as it were, of non-caste, whose principals abrogated those of caste and birth, and the fourth *ashrama* (sanyasa) constituted a door through which the individual was recommended to pass from the world of caste to that of its denial. The mutual relations of the two worlds, and I have no doubt that it was mutual, is of the greatest significance to a full understanding of both.[15] The system of local caste groups predetermined by birth, on the one hand, and the system of voluntaristic cult associations or orders and sects, on the other, cut across one another, forming the essential warp and woof of Hinduism. The third structural feature, kingship, necessary to uphold *varnasrama-dharma*, possessed its own relations with the two contrasting worlds of the Brahman and the sanyasi. Thus the total ideological and social structure of the medieval Hindu world, including its political institution, rested upon a tripartite division and a system of interrelations among the three worlds symbolized by the king, the Brahman and the sanyasi. The domains of *rajya*, *varna grihastha* and of sanyasa formed the three sides of the medieval triangle. The same total structure can perhaps be seen in Islamic civilization of the period in the division and interrelation among the three spheres of *hukumat, shar'iat* and *haqiqat*. These are all problems for future investigation, when broken down into suitable units for study.

An order like the Aghorpanthi jogis, who appear to have smeared themselves with excrements, drunk out of a human skull and occasionally dug up the body of a newly buried child to eat it 'thus carrying out the principle that nothing is common or unclean in its extreme logical conclusion,'[16] evidently constituted the truly living shadow of caste orthodoxy. The theme of antinomian protest could hardly be carried further (unless it was by the Bam-margis who added sexual promiscuity to the list). Yet it could be reliably said of other jogi sub-orders that 'in the Simla hills the Jogis were originally mendicants, but have now become householders', and that the secular jogis, called *sanyogis*, 'in parts of the Punjab form a true caste'.[17] We can resolve this seeming contradiction only if we regard both these jogi conditions as forming the different stages or phases of a single cycle of development. According to this view, we should say that any particular order or sub-order that once renounced caste with all its social rights and duties and walked out into the ascetic wilderness through the front door of sanyasa, could later become disheartened or lose the point of its protest, and even end by seeking to re-enter the house of caste through the backdoor. Of course, as a particular order or section fell back, so to speak, from the frontier of asceticism and abandoned its non-procreative existence without property and occupation. Its function within the total system of *varnasramadharma* would be fulfilled by some other order or section, since the ascetic or protestant impulse itself remained a constant feature. During its ascetic period, an order or sub-order may occupy one or the other of two positions, or pass through them both successively. It may either adopt a theory and practice completely opposed to those of caste, like the Aghorpanthis and Bam-margis, and be, for that reason, regarded as heterodox and esoteric: or it might remain within the pale, and link itself to the caste system through the normal sectarian affiliations of caste people. A 'heterdox' or antinomian sects, we should say, is one opposed to caste as its living shadow: an 'orthodox' is complementary to the caste system, its other half within Hinduism.

As a social movement, the early Sikhism no doubt possessed many features in common with other religious brotherhoods of a certain type. If Sikhism as a whole, nevertheless, broke free from the convoluted cycle of caste *versus* non-caste that overtook other protestant or antinomian brotherhoods, to what cause or causes did it owe its freedom? It is true that Sikhism, as we noted earlier, barred the door of asceticism and so did not lose itself in the esoteric wilderness, but we have also to explain why it did not duly return, as so many others did, to the citadel of caste. The new departure of Sikhism, in my interpretation, was that it set out to annihilate the categorical partitions, intellectual and social, of the medieval world. It rejected the opposition of the common citizen or householder *versus* the renouncer, and the ruler *versus* these two, refusing to acknowledge them as separate and distinct modes of existence. It acknowledged the powers of the three spheres of *rajya*, *sanyasa* and *grihastha*, but sought to invest their virtues conjoinly in a single body of faith and conduct.

The social function of the Sikh initiation rite is, I think, precisely this: to affirm the characteristic rights and responsibilities of the three spheres as equally valid and to invest them as an undivided unit in the neophyte. The new Sikh, therefore, takes no vow to renounce his procreative power by not marrying, instead he dons the *kachha* of continence. Instead of vowing like the jogi never to touch weapons or take other employment or engage in trade, every occupation is, henceforth, open to him, including that of soldiering, maintaining a household or assuming political command. The only thing he is asked to abjure is the degrading practice of begging. The single key of renunciation was thus charged to unlock all dividing doors in the mansion of medievalism. Whether it succeeded, and to what extent, in doing so, is another matter.

The structural method of analysis and interpretation, of which I have attempted to provide an example, shows us that we can establish a definite connection between the five symbols of Sikhism and its whole nature.

If my previous pairing of symbols and the assumption of an unstated term be accepted, the five symbols of Sikhism may be used to signify in this respective pairs the virtues of sanyasa yoga (*kesh* and *kangha*), grihastha yoga (*kachha* and the uncircumcised state) and *rajya yoga* (*kirpan* and *kara*). As the authenticating sign and seal of Sikhism, the five Ks together affirm the unity of man's estate as being all of a piece: this we may take to be the final meaning and function of remaining for ever unshorn in the world. Our analysis would also lead to the conclusion that the total human emancipation of religious man, and not any ideal of a synthesis or reconciliation of Hinduism and Islam, was the faith and endeavour of Sikhism from its inception. The institutionalization of that endeavour surely marked the opening of the modern period of history in the Punjab.

NOTES

1. A noteworthy exception is Kapur Singh, *Parasharprasna, The Baisakhi of Guru Gobind Singh* (Jalandhar: Hind Publishers, 1959), especially Chapters 4 and 5.

2. The material prsented in the succeeding pages is derived from *A Glossary of the Tribes and Castes of the Punjab and North-West Frontier Province* (based on the Census Reports for the Punjab, 1883 and 1892), compiled by H.A. Rose, 3 vols., II, III (Lahore: Samuel T. Weston at Civil and Military Gazette Press, 1911 and 1914). This work is referred to hereinafter as *Punjab Tribes and Castes.*

3. *Punjab Tribes and Castes*, I, 358.

4. P. Hari Kishen Kaul (Punjab Census Report, 1962), quoted in *Punjab Tribes and Castes*, III, 361.

5. The jogis hold the earth and everything made of it in great respect, 'The earthen carpet, the earthen pitcher, the earthen pillar and the earthen roof', is a saying that describes their life. Like the sanyasis, jogis are buried underground and not cremated.

6. *Punjab Tribes and Castes*, II, 400.

7. Ibid., II, 215, where it is also said that other accounts make Dadu contemporary of Dara Shikoh, and still others with Guru Gobind Singh. The *Guru Bilas* gives an interesting story about Guru Gobind Singh's meeting with a Dadupanthi: see Indubhusan Banerjee, *Evolution of the Khalsa*, II (Calcutta: A Mukherjee & Co., 1947, rpt. 1962), 94-5.

8. *Punjab Tribes and Castes*, II. 216.

9. This neglect is apparent, for example, in the work of A. Van Gennep, the French sociologist, *Les rites de passage*, 1908. See English translation by Vizedom and Caffee, *The Rites of Passage* (London: Routledge & Kegan Paul, 1960), p. 97. The same method is followed by Kapur Singh, *Parasharprasna: The Baisakhi of Guru Gobind Singh* (Jalandhar: Hind Publishers, 1959), Chapters 5 and 7.

10. Teja Singh, *Sikhism: Its Ideals and Institutions* (Calcutta: Longmans, Green & Co., 1988), p. 113.

11. *Punjab Tribes and Castes*, II, 86.

12. Ibid., II, 216.

13. Ibid., II, 234

14. M.A. Macauliffe, *The Sikh Religion* (Oxford: Clarendon Press, 1909),V, 99.

15. Caste (and particularly the position of Brahmans) was stated by Max Weber to be 'the fundamental institution of Hinduism'. See H.H. Gerth and C. Wright Mills. From Max Weber, *Essays in Sociology* (London: Routledge & Kegan Paul, 1948), p. 346.

16. This purely one-sided view is especially curious in the German sociologist, since he was the firt to make use (in 1961) of the 'partly excellent scientific Census Reports' (ibid., p. 397) which also form the basis of *Punjab Tribes and Castes* and of the present paper.

17. *Punjab Tribes and Castes*, II, 404.

18. Ibid., II, 399n., 409.

Spiritual Meaning of *Amrit*

P.M. WYLAM

Of all the noble occasions which grace the annals of Sikh history, Baisakhi is the most significant and memorable event. The baptism which Guru Gobind Singh instituted then, was the rebirth and renewal of strength of the whole of the Sikh people, when their solidarity and brotherhood was affirmed and established for all time. In all the versions of the Baisakhi story, none of the Guru's Sikhs thought to question the meaning of, or the need for the five Ks, but now we are in the age of scientific reasoning and research rather than the age of faith and obedience. Now, we must question the Master and try to look for logic in mystical symbols, so we feel the need to appreciate the reasons for the unique symbols and the appropriate instructions which the tenth Guru imparted to our worthy ancestors—his faithful followers at that first Baisakhi gathering in Anandpur in 1699.

The formation of the Khalsa was a natural sequence to and culmination of all that had gone before in the development of the Sikh religion. Guru Nanak's teaching was of brotherly love for all humanity in God's name. He tried to convey, in simple terms, the basic foundation of life and the concept of God making it clear that man and the Universe were indivisibly One. He tried to guide his followers to their own realization and experience of absolute Truth, and to help them free themselves from the continuing rounds of birth and death, with all the attendant human misery. This he tried to do without advocating renunciation or asceticism. He highlighted the fact that remaining in the stream of life and still continuing to act a part in the great divine play was not only possible, but that it was the ideal state to be in.

Guru Gobind Singh demostrated the Guru's teaching by practically applying these principles in his own life. Thus, in a way, he himself acted in the drama. There is no doubt that he played the decisive and dangerous part, yet, in his inner self, he remained detached, God-centered mystic. His poetry reveals his deep devotion to God's name, as well as the love and fatherly care which he not only felt towards the Sikhs, but which he unstintingly bestowed on them. Therefore, it was as their father, the True King and their Guru, that he felt the necessity to bind the Sikhs into one family unit of equal brothers and sisters. They were to throw off all divisions of caste, colour and creed and were to adopt the common surname of 'Singh' for men and 'Kaur' for women. They were to live in the world, but to serve mankind with love and selflessness; they were to strive to realize perfect Divine Unity, both for their own salvation as well as for the service of others. In order to give a realistic meaning to this doctrine, he initiated the ceremony of *amrit* and to ensure a high standard of moral and spiritual behaviour, he laid down certain rules for their guidance. The rules to which the Sikhs were told to adhere:

1. The Khalsa Sikh is to worship one God and to repeat the Sikh prayer, meditating on God's name everyday.
2. He must wear the five symbols (*Panj Kakar*) and he must live according to the rules ordained by the Guru.
3. He must discard his former caste and he must not perform non-Sikh rites and ceremonies, but he must use only Sikh religious ceremonies.
4. He must not commit any of the four misdeeds (*Kurehit*): shaving or cutting the hair, eating meat killed according to Muslim rites (kosher); smoking tobacco, or drinking intoxicants; committing adultery or living immorally.
5. He must contribute one tenth of his income (*dasvand*) for his religion.
6. He must give service to the *sangat*, without expecting anything in return.
7. He must always be ready to defend the weak and to fight in the cause of justice and freedom.

In addition to these obligations, Guru Gobind Singh defines the spiritual characteristics of the Khalsa Sikh in one of his verses:

He who repeats night and day the name of God.
Who has full love and confidence in Him;
Who bestows not a thought on any other but the One God,
Whose enduring light is inextinguishable,
Who puts no faith in fasting or worshipping cemeteries and monasteries,
Who only recognizes the One God and makes no fetish,
Of pilgrimages, alms, charities and austerities:
He is recognized as a true member of the Khalsa
In his heart the light of the Perfect One shines.

Thus with the inauguration of the *amrit* ceremony on Baisakhi day in 1699, Guru Gobind Singh laid the foundation of an earthly organization of the Sikh religion—he thereby formed the body which was intended to house the spirit of the *Guru Granth Sahib.*

It is inevitable that man goes through all the vicissitudes of life while on the Earth. It would not be in the nature of human life if it were otherwise. Therefore, it was in the course of natural events that the Sikhs too, were involved in worldly conflicts from the times of the sixth Guru. These affairs were, however, not an end in themselves because no action was ever undertaken by them for worldly gain; it was all devoted to the cause of the freedom of the spirit. Guru Gobind Singh realized that without striving on the earthly plane, the spiritual battle of the Sikhs would undoubtedly have been lost; the Sikhs must, therefore, be made aware of the obligation to defend their religion against all adversity; but, at the same time, they must neither transgress the natural rights of others or let cruelty and oppression of the innocent be perpetrated by the wicked, however powerful. This was not a departure from the erstwhile principles of Sikhism; it was the necessary and inevitable outcome of the Guru's teaching to live righteously and to serve others. Nevertheless, Guru Gobind Singh emphasized that the sole purpose of religion was spiritual improvement, and the aim of his teaching was to show his followers how to achieve union with God while living a normal life in the world.

Religion, in general, has many aspects and purposes, but there are three things which, in Sikhism, it should set out to achieve. The first is the salvation of the individual: the ennoblement of the soul and its gradual elevation to higher and higher spiritual achievement until it attains Oneness with God.

The second aim of Sikhism is the improvement of society; the collective welfare of humanity through the working of the Khalsa brotherhood. This also serves the individual, for by fellowship with others, who are striving in the same direction, the brother gets encouragement and moral support.

The third function of Sikhism is to transcend the obstacles which are placed by most religions as regards people who do not conform to the tenets of their own religions. Sikh religion is, therefore, a natural refuge for such excluded people—a spiritual home for the homeless, so that those wandering souls who have failed to find a place elsewhere in the human family should find it with the Khalsa and, by the aid of the Guru's teaching, become transformed from aimless children into confident manhood. Although the Khalsa brotherhood itself consists of the strong in spirit, it does not forsake the weak. These latter are not admitted to its ranks as a matter of course, but matters are so organized that every help is given to satiating the spiritual hunger as it increases.

Some people argue that these aims can be achieved without the Sikh having to wear the five symbols, and so, what is the purpose in adhering to them? Taken collectively, the five Ks are a common denominator binding the Sikhs together into a brotherhood of people, all striving to reach the same religious objectives. By wearing the symbols, the Sikhs all resemble their Master (their spiritual father) and they also resemble each other, as brothers of the same family. The symbols also serve the purpose of a uniform, which, history has shown, is the basic element for infusing the spirit of oneness and of purpose in any army.

Taken individually, the symbols have great significance, for they represent, outwardly, the qualities which the Sikh should cultivate inwardly, and by keeping them on his person the Sikh is helped in his resolve to cultivate them in his soul.

Kesh

The uncut hair represents the complete, natural person. When the body is whole, in the form that God made, then it represents also the whole spirit—the spirit unlimited by worldly considerations. The hair is cut because of vanity or because of a wish to conform to the worldly norm. To defy this norm shows freedom of spirit and non-attachment to the world. Most people exist, being only partly and dimly aware of themselves; their minds are not fully conscious, and they are quite unaware of the divinity within. The Sikh must try to become fully conscious, and he must try to be aware of the whole of his inner and real self. Thus, his soul, like his body, will become whole and complete. The same principle of wholeness is equally applied to the rest of the human body in Sikhism.

Kangha

In the same way the comb keeps the hair tidy, grooms it, keeps the knot firmly in place, so the comb symbolizes the discipline of the mind. By wearing the comb the Sikh should be reminded to keep his mind under control; his thoughts should not be allowed to wander aimlessly, but his mind should be kept orderly, methodical and well-disciplined. The spirit, through intuition, should rule the intellect, and the intellect should rule the emotions. Thus excessive anger or excessive attachment will be avoided.

Kachha

By adopting the shorts, it was intended to symbolize the spiritual and mental breakaway from the traditional dress and thought. The mind was to be freed from the bonds of superstitious beliefs, and Sikhs were thus to be released from immature and effeminate submissiveness. They were destined to become mature, solid and active soldiers. They were also to be self-controlled, chaste and chivalrous. Since the symbol of the *kachha* was the same for Sikh women, they were also intended to develop the same qualities as Sikh men.

Kirpan

The short sword is the symbol of freedom from oppression and servility. Its obvious meaning was for self-defence and the individual freedom and self-respect embodied in the right to bear arms. The deeper, spiritual meaning of the *kirpan* is that it is symbolic of the triumph of transcendental knowledge over ignorance and darkness. The sword, in the mind, cuts at the roots of ignorance, evil and worldly attachment and destroys them utterly.

Kara

The steel bangle binds the Sikh with a strong unbreakable link, to his religion, to the Khalsa and his Sikh brothers. The complete, unbroken circle symbolizes the unbroken continuity of existence. Life is not something which began in the past, exists for a while and ends at some time in the future. The spiritual reality of life exists continually, free of both time and space. All appearances are subject to change, but change is only on the surface, like ripples in the ocean. No point on the circumference of a circle can be called the beginning or the end of it, so by wearing the bangle, the Sikh is reminded to cultivate in himself the awareness of immortality and timelessness. Steel itself is symbolic, since it is strong yet resilient under stress. In the same way, the human soul must become as strong and unbreakable as steel which has been tempered in the furnace.

A Sikh who takes *amrit* and wears the five symbols, even if at first, he does not fully comprehend their significance, naturally comes under their beneficent spiritual influence. It is true that an Amritdhari Sikh may still fall from grace if either he does not make the necessary spiritual effort within himself, or if he fails to maintain it; and he may wear the symbols as a hypocrite, outwardly but not inwardly. For this lapse, no one can blame the rules of the Khalsa. It is not unknown for material fabricated to the most rigid specifications to fall under stress and even fatigue. Man is a victim of environmental, physical, social, domestic and economic stresses. He can advance a hundred-and-one excuses for his own shortcomings. The soul of man is a spark from God's own pure light; but because it is encased in a body which may or may not have developed to its fullest potential, it is like a light imprisoned in a glass bottle. If the glass is clean and pure, the light will shine through it and illuminate the world, but if the glass is naturally clouded or dirty within, the brilliance of the light will be obscured. Our Gurus have had over 200 years of continuous and unbroken experience of human evolution and as a result of that experience they evolved spiritual principles and rules of guidance which, if followed with sincerity and conviction, are true for all time. Either through lack of matching experience, or through faulty approach, we sometimes fail to attain the standard laid down. The mind, being a dynamic force, and the pattern of human behaviour being generally unpredictable, it is difficult for different individuals to have uniformity of approach. It is for this reason that while sometimes the councils and committees of the Sikh *sangats* come to be headed by those who truly strive to reveal the light, and the Khalsa really becomes the community of saints which the great Guru created, yet we also have numerous occasions of the opposite, when the aspirations of the Sikh community are not fulfilled. The Sikhs are nevertheless fully conscious of their own shortcomings and even in their ·personal failures they realize that in order that all their works be blessed and the projects which they plan bear fruit and become successful, they will have to strive hard, with all the goodwill and brotherly love at their command. The words of Guru Gobind Singh always echo in the subconscious of their minds:

He has no lust, wrath, covetousness,
or worldly love or sickness, sorrow, enjoyment or fear.
He is without a body, He has love for all,
yet He is devoid of sensual love.
He is homeless and indestructible.
To those who know Him, He gives,
even to those who do not know Him, He gives.

He gives to the earth; He gives to the heaven.
O man, why do you hesitate?
The beautiful and holy Lord of
wealth will take care of you.

Guru Gobind Singh, *Swayya* 5

The Five Sikh Symbols

J.S. NEKI

Any study of religious symbols involves a dual task; firstly to explain the meaning of symbols not only in terms of their original connotations but also on the basis of contemporary categories of understanding; secondly to discriminate between genuine symbolism and any *post hoc* interpretations which in later times may have imposed on things originally having little symbolic relevance.

Like any other religion, Sikhism also incorporates in its thought and practice a variety of symbols. *Nam* (the Holy Name), *Hukam* (the Divine Order), *Maya* (the Cosmic Illusion), *Kal* (the Mortifying Time), *Akal* (the Reality that transcends Time), among several others, represent one order of symbols, viz., the theological thought. Another order of symbols operates at the level of formal practice. *Amrit Sanchar* (the baptismal initiating ceremony) is the most outstanding of these and has been styled after the original ceremony that canonized the order of the Khalsa (AD 1699).

During the baptismal ceremony every initiate of the order, *inter alia*, is enjoined upon to wear and keep on his person five symbolic physical items designated as *kakars* (so called because their names begin with the phoneme 'K'). These by convention include *kesh* (unshorn hair), *kangha* (a comb), *kirpan* (a sword), *kara* (a steel bangle) and *kachha* (a pair of specially styled shorts).

Some relevant texts (e.g. *Sarab Loh Granth*), record that only three of these five symbols (colletivelly called *Traimudra* (the symbolic triad) had, in fact, been ordained initially. These three were *kesh*, *kirpan*, and *kachha*. In that case, *klangha* and *kara* must have got included later. One reason advanced for this is that the numeral 'five' had come to acquire a special mystical significance in Sikh parlance (based perhaps on the scriptural proclamation: *Panjin Parmeshar*, i.e. among the five, God Himself exists. The number might also have been favoured because it harmonized with the other 'fives' in the baptismal ceremony—the *Panj*

Piare (Five Loved Ones) and *Panj Banian* (the five scriptural texts prescribed for daily recitation). Another conjecture has been that the elevation of the number of these symbols from three to five might have been occasioned by the desire to fully countermatch the Nath yogis' *Panj Makars* (symbols originating with the phoneme 'M'). The *Bhatt Vahis* providing an almost contemporary evidence, however, record that five symbols, indeed, had been ordained *ab initio*, but list *kesgi* (turban) in place of *kesh* (vide infra).

It seems to be essential for a social symbol to contain something of the nature of an archetypal kernel. That is how it appeals to the collective consciousness of the community and thereby acquires wide acceptance and emotional sway over minds of men.

Kesh (the unshorn hair) have a dual, investing and a divesting, significance. On the one hand it seems to emboss the investiture of the spiritual man (exemplified by *rishis*, *avatars*) and even of God Himself (whose epithet Keshav means one who wears long hair) upon the initiate. On the other hand, unshorn hair also signify manliness, virility, courage and dignity. The *kesh*, therefore, also spell the investiture of honour and valour.

They also seem to have a divestural function—in that they countermand renunciation of the world and asceticism which are symbolized among certain cults by trichodilapidatory rituals.

The wearing of unshorn hair, therefore, symbolizes for the Sikhs at once a life of spiritual devotion (*bhakti*) and of strength (*shakti*) of conviction, of courage and of fortitude.

Kangha (the comb), required to keep the hair tidy, came to symbolize cleanliness, which, here clearly stands next to godliness. As a divestural symbol, it appears to repudiate the practices of tantric yogis, the outward symbol of whose denominations is matted hair (*jata*).

Kirpan (the sword) signifies worship through valour. It seems to represent what has been called 'the Sword of God in heavenly regions'. also called *Bhagauti* in Sikh parlance (which expression stands for the 'Sword' as well as for the 'Almighty'), it is invoked in the very beginning of the Sikh prayer, *Ardas*.

The word *kirpan* seems to have been compounded from *kirpa* (compassion) and *an* (dignity). Hence, it is a weapon that shall only be wielded in compassion (to protect the oppressed) and for upholding human dignity. It stands, therefore, for the heroic affirmation of a valorous life of dignity for the vindication of ethical principles.

Kara (the steel bangle) was in vogue as a pragmatic accessory to the *kirpan.* A set of strong steel bangles used to be worn by warriors as protective armour over the arm that wielded the sword. But besides the symbolism of self-defence that its pragmatic value seems to indicate, it has a keener symbolic significance in its shape, i.e. that of a circle. A circle signifies perfection, without a beginning and without an ending. In traditional Indian symbolism a circle also represents *Dharma*, Supreme Law, and Divine Justice. It also symbolizes perfect restraint. The *kara*, therefore, symbolizes for the Sikhs a just and lawful life of self-discipline (*Rahit*) and self-control (*sanjam*).

Kachha (pair of shorts) is a sartorial symbol signifying manly reserve in the commitment of procreative function. In this, it stands to repudiate puritanical vows of chastity (of the Hindu sanyasa) as also the Muslim practice of circumcision.

At the pragmatic level, its sartorial design makes for greater agility and ease of movement of the lower limbs—thereby facilitating a state of unhindred readiness—*tayyar bar tayyar* (literally, readiness beyond ordinary readiness).

Of these five symbols, *kesh* seems to have the primary position. Causing injury to one's hair is a proscriptive taboo (*Kurehit*) for the Sikhs. 'Without unshorn hair the other four lose their significance.' The Sikhs, therefore, have great respect for their hair. They have not only desisted from cropping them, but have insisted on their tidiness, doing them up into a neat vertical knot and draping them with a shapely turban. Wearing a turban had been proclaimed the exclusive prerogative of the Muslim ruling class during the early days of the Khalsa. The turban for the Sikhs was, therefore, a symbolic proclamation against curtailment of civic liberties. Simultaneously, it also signified for the Sikhs their identity. As alluded to earlier, the Bhatt Vahis actually report *kesgi* (the turban) among the five *Kakars* ordained to be observed.

The Sikhs, over a long stretch of their history, suffered intense persecution at the hands of bigoted Muslim rulers. They were hunted out and those captured were sought to be divested of their hair on the pain of death. History testified that the Sikhs, by and large, preferred death to dilapidatory apostasy. It is during such times that the Sikhs introduced into their prayer, *Ardas* or a petitional phrase invoking the Lord to ensure preservation of their sacred hair until their last breath (*Sikhi Kesan Swasan Sang Nibhani*).

Historically again, time after time, the powers that be, imposed restrictions on the religious right of the Sikhs to carry a *kirpan* on their person. The community always agitated against such restrictive orders. It is during some such times that a phrase invoking the mighty assistance of

Sri Sahib (as this consecrated weapon was reverently called) got included in their prayer.

Thus, these symbols, over and above their original connotations, came to signify, through historical vicissitudes, the distinctive identity and collective aspirations of the Sikh people.

These symbols, being the gift of the Guru, also possess a sacramental status. They are held dear as keepsakes of the tenth Guru who sacrificed all that was his for the Khalsa. A keepsake essentially symbolizes a relationsship of love. These symbols, therefore, also signify the Sikhs' love for their Guru as also his for them.

The Symbols of a Heritage

I.J. SINGH

'History', as T.S. Eliot said, 'has many cunning passages, contrived corridors and issues. . . .' Insofar as religions deal with people, places and events, they are amenable to historical analyses. But religion deals with a reality that transcends history—a reality that the senses cannot perceive and the intellect cannot fathom, yet with which the soul can commune. At that point in awareness, one is in the domain of faith. Faith is better than belief. In belief, someone else does the thinking for you; in faith, you accept the truth not at someone else's says-so, but because you have internalized it and endorsed it. Belief can mature into faith. From belief comes dependency; from faith, strength. The intangible realm of faith is a symbolic reality that is best expressed through symbols.

It would be worthwhile remembering that the dimension of faith is not that of science. Of man's many concerns, the deepest faith is symbolically expressed. By definition, symbols and signs signify something else beyond themselves, yet a symbol participates in defining the reality to which it points. A flag is not a nation but a symbol of it and attests to the shared history and dignity of a nation. That is why good people will fight and die for a flag but not let it be desecrated; it becomes significantly more in worth than the price of the cloth from which it is cut. A symbol, therefore, cannot be easily replaced by another, or be subjected to scientific logic, nor can it be judged by the criteria of the marketplace.

Symbols are seen in every act of faith. They live and die but only after a historical catastrophe which greatly alters a people's perception of self and their destiny. The death of existing symbols constitutes devastating events no less important than the phenomena that give them birth and shape. Symbols cannot be invented at will or intentionally produced by committees like business logos. They grow out of the collective consciousness of a people and have to be accepted by the subconscious dimension of their being. Their majesty and power lies in their symbolic character, not in any utilitarian value they might possess. Symbols are found in most aspects of man's creative activity—art, music, mathematics, history, religion, etc. In fact, man's cultural history is often symbolically expressed. A cross is a symbol of Christ's suffering, not the reality of it. After 2,000 years of the diaspora, the Jews seem to have recognized how symbols connect people to their roots; witness the growing popularity of the Lubavitchers.

India has produced many new religions—Buddhism, Jainism, Sikhism, among others. Of these, only Sikhs remains as a visible, active and distinct entity; others have reverted into the uneasy but comforting fold of Hinduism. Buddhism remains a powerful presence in Sri Lanka, Thailand, Myanmar, Vietnam, China and Japan, but not in the land of its birth—India.

John Kenneth Galbraith is correct in his somewhat facetious observation that anything that goes to India or develops there eventually gets Hinduized. He was talking of industry but it is equally true of religions. Islam in India is not quite the same as it is elsewhere, nor is Christianity. Sikhism too has lost some of its lustre and much of its pristine purity by its constant encounters with Hinduism. If Sikhism has not been absorbed into the Hindu fold entirely, it is not for want of trying by Hindus, but due to two reasons: (a) its distinct philosophy which is at odds with and bluntly scornful of many Hindu practices, but that is a minor factor in its survival since most Sikhs are not well versed in it, and (b) the distinct external symbols of Sikhism which set the Sikhs apart in appearance and behaviour.

Sometimes, I think that the rot in Sikhism had set in, but has been checked somewhat by the dramatic trauma to their psyche that occurred when the Indian army attacked the Golden Temple and many other gurdwaras in 1984. In many ways, those events and the subsequent frictions between the Indian Government and the Sikhs has forced most Sikhs to re-examine their values and their sense of self. Many Sikhs who were no longer recognizable, became so by readopting the symbols of their faith. It was a horrendous price to pay for the Sikhs, but in the longer historical perspective, the benefits may be an increased self-awareness.

The most visible aspects of Sikh tradition, and the most controversial are the external symbols. Not surprisingly, they generate the most intense internal debate and external concern. The interesting point is that only in Sikhism are such weighty and important matters debated by such levity. It is like 'war being too important to be left to the Generals'. The theologians and the clergy may preach and teach but the discussion is led and fueled by the ordinary folks who have to live the religion in the modern world, these people are on the frontlines and know the price, the problems, the frustrations as well as the rewards. And many of the people have never even taken the final vows (*amrit*) of becoming Sikhs. It was just as true at the time of Guru Gobind Singh as it is now that many Sikhs never adopted all of the symbols of Sikhism but—like the Marrano Jews—kept their faith. Such Sehajdhari Sikhs have occupied an important and honorable place in Sikh history.

There are many ways to look at Sikh symbols, the most popular way is to say: the Guru ordained them, ours is not to question why or what he meant by them. There is merit in that position. But the Guru did not bar us from thinking, so let us see what history can tell us. If symbols emerge out of shared history, how did we come to these five? And how has history affected them?

The Sikh with his external uniform and symbols is a Khalsa, a soldier in the army of God. This army created by Guru Gobind Singh was not made to rule over others or to shepherd a flock of sheep-like devotees. Unlike the army of Christ, where only the clergy were to be in uniform, in this army of the Khalsa, all followers were to join, all were to wear the uniform, everyone was always on call.

Though symbols are not to be judged by their utilitarian value, some of the Sikh symbols seem to be more functional than others. If long hair is *de rigueur*, a comb is essential for grooming, particularly for a people who knew no peace and lived on horseback. For a people fighting for survival, a sword as a weapon ensured survival. Again, befitting their lifestyle and India's terrain and weather, knee-length drawers were appropriate. A steel bracelet spoke of the strength of steel; its circle of a life with no beginning and no end. This strong wide band of steel could also protect or be used as a weapon. In seventeenth century India, when there was a price on every Sikh's head, when a non-Muslim could not wear a turban, carry a weapon or ride a horse, when it was easier and more tempting to join the faceless anonymous hordes, the long-haired Khalsa boldly asserted their presence through their visible symbols. These symbols were a uniform of the Khalsa and still remain so. The philosophy of the Khalsa is eternal and the symbols represent it.

When I look at these symbols nearly three hundred years later, I see that most Sikhs have made a distinction even though at a subconscious level and look at symbols in two different tiers. Circumstances and times have indeed changed. The sword, the comb and the knee-length drawers were primarily utilitarian and seem to have changed the most with time. The sword that most Sikhs carry nowadays has been reduced to a symbolic level. Sometimes it is a dull blade a few inches long; more often it is a symbolic sword no more than an inch or two long attached to a comb or a pendent; at times it is only an impression of the sword inlaid into the wood of the comb. The sword has changed from a practical instrument of defence to a symbolic presence of that principle, of strength and resoluteness in action. Similarly, the knee-length drawers which were the only garment worn below a loose, long shirt have been modified by most Sikhs who wear the conventional underwear to go with other street attire. The comb though utilitarian has not changed all that much because it is still necessary for the long hair, although many Sikh women now carry only a small non functional miniature.

The steel bracelet and the long hair remain what they have always been—strictly symbolic. Professor Puran Singh likened the steel bracelet to a wedding band signifying the marriage of the Sikh to the Guru. However, a marriage is a sacrament only where there is a real love; for many philanderers the bracelet, like the wedding band, can come on or off with equal ease. Others would rather lose a finger, a hand or a head than a wedding band. A Sikh surgeon would need to remove it and pocket it lest it tears the gloves. If the identity of a Sikh depended only on a visible bracelet, it would be easy for one to hide and that is not what Guru Gobind Singh intended. The long unshorn hair, strictly symbolic, with no pragmatic use or value in the market place remains the centerpiece of Sikh identity. It was true 300 years ago and remains equally true now.

One wonders what circumstances in history mandated that only the men adopt the turban to cover their long hair and not the women. The women do maintain all the Sikh symbols including the long unshorn hair. But in the Indian cultural milieu, without a turban they are not easily distinguishable from the millions of Indian women who are not Sikh. Certainly there is no bar to women wearing a turban and some Sikh women in India do; almost all the Western converts to Sikhism do. For women, wearing the turban over their long hair appears to have less to do with their understanding of Sikhism and more to do with the cultural constraints or with the particular school of thought or teacher who has influnced them. One need also remember that around the time that the Sikh symbols evolved, the Muslim rulers had barred non-Muslim men from wearing a turban. In the Indian culture, the turban for a man signified respect, irrespective of religion, women did not wear it. It was worn by a man who mattered and at that time, the emphasis of the rulers was to debase the subjects and deny them basic human dignity, self-worth and self-respect. The Gurus reversed this process and the turban, though not one of the five basic symbols of Sikhism, became inseparable from them, at least for the men.

To serve well, symbols must remain visible. Sometimes they are hidden much as the Marrano Jews found it necessary to hide their Jewishness when survival demanded it. Sikh symbols too can be easily concealed—all except the long, unshorn hair. That is precisely why in the annals of Sikh history, the unshorn hair have commanded the highest value. I don't know if Guru Gobind Singh so intended but in the subconscious dimension of their being, the Sikhs have somehow created a hierarchy of their symbols; the long unshorn hair has come to occupy the place of first among equals. A Sikh historically and now, declares his presence by this gift of his Guru. This is wholly consistent with the philosophic significance of a Sikh, and I venture to say that no matter how Sikhs change and what demands are placed upon them, as long as there are those who call themselves Sikhs, there will be long haired Sikhs in the form that Guru Gobind Singh gave them. The dictum on the interdependence of form and function is significant and worthy of our attention.

A person gets from a symbol what he puts in it. It can be one man's comfort and inspiration as easily as another's jest and scorn. In the final analysis, symbols are an embodiment of history, not sentiment.

Sikhs and the Turban

W.H. MCLEOD

In 1925 the Government of the Punjab brought five years of Sikh agitation to a close with the passing of the Sikh Gurdwaras Act. The agitation concerned the control of Sikh gurdwaras (or 'temples') and the Act, which is still essentially in force, was crucial in the history and definition of the Sikh community (the Panth). It was crucial in that it defined in very specific terms who is a Sikh. The Act, it is true, represented the victory of one of the two main groups within the Panth over the other. It is abundantly clear, however, that the view it represents is that of the portion of the Panth which has unquestionably established itself as orthodox. It is the view of practically all outsiders. The Act defines a Sikh as follows:

I solemnly affirm that I am a Sikh, that I believe in the *Guru Granth Sahib*, that I believe in the Ten Gurus, and that I have no other religion.[1]

All those who qualify under this definition affirm what the West calls Sikhism and what Sikhs themselves usually refer to as *Gurmat*, i.e. 'the teachings of the Guru'.[2] This involves belief in one God, in the divine mission of ten Gurus, in the sanctity of the Sikh scripture (the *Guru Granth Sahib*), and in the role of the community known as the Khalsa. It is the last of these four articles which causes some who regard themselves as Sikhs to disagree. Those who dissent are, however, only a small minority. They are distinct from the overwhelming majority who accept that the Khalsa has a central and vital role to play in the life of the Panth. It is the majority whose claims to orthodoxy are unassailable.

GURU NANAK AND THE FOUNDING OF THE SIKH PANTH

All Sikhs acknowledge Nanak (1469-1539), first of the ten Gurus, as founder of their faith. 'Sikh' means 'learner' and the first Sikhs were the followers whom Guru Nanak attracted to his Nanakpanth or 'the way of Nanak'. Little can be known about his life with assurance except in bare outline. Extensive accounts known as *Janam-sakhis* ('birth testimonies') certainly exist, but these represent hagiographic anecdotes circulated by Nanak's later followers and are altogether untrustworthy as biography. His teachings, however, are well documented.

Nanak was born a Hindu in Talvandi (now called Nanakana Sahib), a village situated 40 miles west of Lahore. His father Mehta Kalu agreed to send him to the Punjab town of Sultanpur Lodhi where he was employed in the local ruler's commissariat. While there, he is said to have had a vision which led him to undertake extensive travels, preaching the message of the divine Name. Eventually he settled in the Punjab village of Kartarpur where he died in 1539.

His teachings centred on belief in the *nam* (the divine Name) by which is meant everything that can be comprehended concerning *Akal Purakh* (God). *Akal Purakh* is formless, yet His wonders are to be seen everywhere. Open your eyes, says Nanak, and you shall see Him, both in the world around you and within. These wonders testify to the unchanging purpose of *Akal Purakh*. Meditate on this, turn your whole life towards Him in a regular daily discipline of 'remembering the divine Name' (*Nam Simaran*), and gradually you will attain a final harmony of spirit. This is the path of liberation, the way in which the wheel of endless death and rebirth ultimately ceases to revolve as the soul reaches perfect peace.

This method of deliverance was one open to all men and women, regardless of their deeds in past existences or their caste in this. It was also one which could be followed without separating oneself from the world. Above all else, the practice was wholly internal, without any need of external objects. The only necessary thing is meditation. This could be simple repetition of sacred words such as *Sat Nam* (true is the Name) or *Waheguruji* (the popular modern name amongst Sikhs for God); it could be singing works of the Guru; or it could be deep interior meditation.

The teachings of Nanak are commonly misunderstood as a blend of Hindu and Muslim beliefs. This is far from the truth. For Nanak the beliefs and practices of both the Hindu and the Muslim could be either true or false. They were true if they upheld remembrance of the divine name within; and they were astray if they put their faith in anything external— in temples, mosques, idols, pilgrimage, or sacred scriptures.

Is Sikhism therefore merely one of the many varieties of Hindu tradition? The Nanakpanth was believed to transcend India's traditional religion, but in the time of the early Gurus there was nothing which marked Nanak's Sikhs out as clearly separate. Only later, with the establishment of the Khalsa by Guru Gobind Singh, did a portion of the Panth become outwardly and visibly unique. Warfare with Muslims in the eighteenth century persuaded the Sikhs that they certainly were not followers of Islam; and with the birth of the Singh Sabha movement towards the end of the nineteenth century many Sikhs were likewise convinced that they were not Hindus either. Most Sikhs now believe that they are neither Muslim nor Hindu. They are a separate religious community, unmistakably distinct.

THE LATER GURUS AND THE FOUNDING OF THE KHALSA

Before he died, Nanak appointed as his successor loyal disciple Angad (1539-52), second Guru of the Sikhs. Angad was followed by Amar Das (1552-74), during whose period the Panth underwent a process of consolidation. The Panth needed a more coherent organization and this Amar Das provided with festivals, a pilgrimage centre, and a collection of hymns. Amar Das was followed by his son-in-law Ram Das (1574-81), distinguished for his hymns and for building the sacred centre of Amritsar. He was succeeded by his own son Arjan (1581-1606) who compiled the *Adi Granth*. The collection of hymns irked of the rulers of northern India, the Mughals, and Arjan thus became the first martyr-Guru.

This event prompted a change of policy under Arjan's son and successor. Hargobind (1606-44) took up arms and skirmished with Mughal forces. Under the two following Gurus, Har Rai (1644-61) and the child Guru Har Krishan (1661-4), the situation remained relatively quiet, but the ninth Guru Tegh Bahadur (1664-75), became the second martyr to die at the hands of the Mughals.

During the lifetime of all the Gurus the Punjab was under Mughal rule. The Mughals were in command of the Punjab plains, with the foothills of the Himalayas ruled by several semi-independent chieftains who acknowledged Mughal sovereignty. The tenth and last Guru Gobind Singh (1675-1708), took a momentous step in 1699. He summoned his Sikhs to Anandpur and there he inaugurated the order of the Khalsa.

The Khalsa was evidently aimed, in part at least, at those Sikhs who gave allegiance to corrupt deputies of the Guru (the *masands*). It was, however, more than this. All Sikhs who became members were to owe unconditional loyalty directly to the Guru. Entry was by baptism and it included only those Sikhs who were prepared to be recognized (their hair was to remain uncut) and to bear arms in a firm determination to fight for their faith. Gobind Singh delivered to his Khalsa a simple *Rahit* or code of conduct. Today Sikhs of the Khalsa observe the five Ks as the central part of the *Rahit*, so called because each begins with the letter 'k'. These are the *kesh* (uncut hair), the *kangha* (wooden comb), the *kara* (iron bangle), the *kirpan* (sword or dagger), and the *kachha* (a pair of shorts which must not come below the knees). Membership is open to both men and women, the former adopting Singh as a second name and the latter assuming the name Kaur.

The difference between Khalsa and non-Khalsa Sikhs is crucial to any understanding of the Sikhs and Sikhism, though the distinctions within the Panth are actually more complex than this suggests. At one extreme of the Panth are the Amritdhari Sikhs, those who have received *amrit* (water of baptism) and are full-fledged members of the Khalsa. Next to them come the Keshdhari Sikhs, not necessarily initiated members of the Khalsa but ideally bearing its outward symbols and certainly the uncut hair. At the other extreme are the Sahajdhari Sikhs who revere the Gurus and scripture but do not observe the *Rahit*. Sahajdharis are not members of the Khalsa. In between (without a name to distinguish them) are those from a Khalsa background who cut their hair. Many of this group would want to claim Khalsa membership, but it seems they must be excluded. We shall return to these groups later in this paper.

SUBSEQUENT SIKH HISTORY

Shortly before he died Guru Gobind Singh declared that the line of personal Gurus would end with his death, the function of Guru thereafter being expressed jointly by the sacred scripture (which came to be known as the *Guru Granth Sahib*) and by the Panth. During the eighteenth century, Punjab lived through tumultuous times, with the Sikhs gradually establishing political dominance. During the first five decades of the nineteenth century, Punjab was ruled by the Sikhs, the first four under Maharaja Ranjit Singh. Their number, however, was never more than a small proportion of the total population. In 1849, the Sikh kingdom was annexed by the British and many people believed that Sikhism was doomed to extinction. It was saved from this by the rise of the Singh Sabha movement, founded in 1873.

Although its principal effect was exercised between 1890 and 1920 the Singh Sabha continues informally to be a strong influence within the Panth. Two distinct groups emerged in the Singh Sabha—the conservative Sanatan Sikhs and the radical *Tat Khalsa* (the 'Pure Khalsa'). Whereas the former claimed that Sikhs were merely another variety of Hindus, the latter vehemently opposed this. Eventually the *Tat Khalsa* secured dominance, insisting that their interpretation of the faith was correct and that Sikhism is a completely separate religion. It is not possible to estimate what proportion of the entire Panth agrees with this view today, but there can be no doubt that it is accepted by a large majority of the Khalsa.

THE GURDWARA AND THE *GURU GRANTH SAHIB*

The Gurdwara or temple is the centre of the Sikh faith, today as in centuries past. There the *Guru Granth Sahib* is the object of intense devotion, each person bowing before it upon entry. The Sikhs have no clergy and anyone in good standing in the Panth can lead the worship which consists largely of singing hymns from the Sikh scripture. Each Gurdwara must have a *langar* (free refectory) where anyone, regardless of religion, colour or caste, can dine. There can be no doubt that Sikhism has abolished caste within the gurdwara. Outside the gurdwara the practice is generally continued, at least as far as marriage is concerned, but the scholarly view within the community is that this retention is merely for social adherence. It is not essential to the faith—far from it. A majority of Sikhs actually belong to the Jat caste, the dominant rural caste in the Punjab.

MODERN SIKHS AND SIKHISM

Sikhs have long been noted as a warrior community, a role which the British learnt to respect in the two Anglo-Sikh wars of the 1840 and which they turned to practical purpose by a policy of extensive Sikh recruitment in the army of British India. The Sikhs are also noted for overseas migration, travelling to South-East Asia and Australia in the 1880s and to North America just after 1900.[3] Since 1947 the numbers have greatly increased and there are now believed to be approximately one million Sikhs living outside India (particularly in England). On the whole the migrants have done well economically and have lavished much generosity on their gurdwaras. As yet there is little sign that the faith has significantly changed in response to its new circumstances.

THE ORIGIN AND IMPORTANCE OF THE
WARRIOR ROLE IN SIKHISM

Sikhism was born in the Punjab, a territory which has been crossed on countless occasions by armies and armed bands out of Central Asia, using the Khyber Pass as the only suitable means of access into India. This, after all, was the route used by the early Indo-Aryans who began their descent about two and a half millennia BC and since their arrival on the plains of India numerous other invaders have followed them. Not until the Europeans arrived by sea at the end of the fifteenth century did invaders come by sea, and even then it was not until the eighteenth century that the Europeans began serious conquest.

The eighteenth century emphasizes the importance of the Punjab as a route for invaders, for during the period the Persians came down the Khyber Pass once and the Afghans invaded northern India no less than nine times. The Punjab has obviously been the scene of frequent tumult for innumerable centuries and it comes as no surprise to learn that the adaptive groups in Punjabi society conspicuously include those people who have learnt to defend themselves. The most conspicuous of all these people are the Jats, the dominant caste in rural Punjab. The Jats, as we have already noted, constitute an absolute majority of all Sikhs. The precise proportion is not known, but in the days of the British census-taking the figure was approximately 66 per cent and it is clear that of the Sikhs today the Jats must number at least 60 per cent.

None of the Sikh Gurus were Jats (they were all Khatris by caste), but the reason why the Jats were attracted to their message is surely evident. Because they dirtied their hands with agriculture the Jats rated low on the traditional caste scale. They were certainly not outcaste, but they nevertheless occupied an inferior rung on the caste ladder. This lowliness contrasted with the increasingly significant influence which they commanded in the villages of the Punjab, and it made them very receptive to the egalitarian message preached by the Gurus. The Gurus taught that caste made not a scrap of difference to one's hope of liberation, nor did the claims of privilege lodged by these groups such as the Brahmans. All were based upon mere externals. True liberation was wholly dependent upon what lay within a person and internally all were equal. The outcast had every bit as much hope as the Brahman.

This message fell upon receptive ears in the case of the Jats and soon they were flocking to join the new Nanakpanth. Although for the first two centuries the leadership continued to be largely Khatri the actual membership was predominantly Jat. By becoming a Sikh, however, the Jat did not cease to be a Jat. This was far from being the case. The Jat had for generations past been nurtured in the need for defence and if necessary to convert defence into vigorous attack. For the Jat the trusted means of looking after himself was his own strong arm, and Jat men at least would rarely be at large without at least a solid staff or preferably a sword.

This warrior spirit the Jats carried with them into the Panth and because they were the dominant group within the Panth. It may have been the simplest of interpretations which rural folk placed upon the message, but it was the Gurus' message which they accepted and upon the individual Gurus they bestowed the most profound respect.

During the eighteenth century the Sikhs were assailed by Mughals and Afghans, and they fought for their lives in conditions which exalted the warrior spirit. Eventually they emerged to supremacy in the Punjab under Maharaja Ranjit Singh at the beginning of the nineteenth century. Ranjit Singh created what was regarded as the strongest army in Asia next to the British. After his death the army provided the British with some very hard-fought battles and, as we have seen, after the Punjab had been annexed in 1849 the British expressed their considerable respect for the Sikh fighting spirit by recruitment into their Indian army. In so doing the British required their Sikh soldiers to remain visibly Sikh, maintaining as their uniform at all times (including in battle) the distinctive Sikh turban. Some Sikh regiments wore their regimental badges on their turbans.

Today the same spirit lives on except that Sikh recruitment has fallen. Quotas based on regions have led the Indian Government to reduce Sikh recruitment, to the continuing indignation of the Khalsa. Recruitment, say the Khalsa Sikhs, should be based on suitability, not on regional quotas. Several personal names with obvious military connotations are still used by Sikhs. Fauja recalls the army (fauj means 'army'), and Karnail and Jarnail are actual ranks (being Punjabi forms of the English 'colonel' and 'general'). Associated with the military process is a considerable interest and achievement in sport. In this respect also the Sikh record has been a notable one.

THE FIVE Ks, AND THE DEFINITION OF SIKH ORTHODOXY

The five Ks (*Panj Kakar* or *Panj Kake*) are the five external symbols which, as we have noted, all Khalsa Sikhs should wear. They are so called because each begins with 'k'. The five are *kesh* or *kesha* (uncut hair), *kangha* (comb), *kara* (or steel ring round the wrist), *kirpan* (sword or dagger), and *kachha* or *kachhahra* (shorts which must not come below the knee).

Tradition records that these five symbols were conferred by Guru Gobind Singh upon all who accepted initiation into the Khalsa when first it was inaugurated in 1699. As such they form a key part of the *Rahit* or the 'Code of Conduct' promulgated by the Guru in 1699. For those who take initiation they are regarded as absolutely mandatory. Keshdharis are also expected to maintain them.

As we have already seen, those who take initiation are known as

Amritdhari Sikhs, *amrit* being the water with which they are baptised. Amritdhari Sikhs are actually a relatively small portion of the Khalsa, being joined in this respect by a much more substantial number of Keshdhari Sikhs. Keshdhari Sikhs are literally those who do not cut their *kesh* (hair). Frequently they maintain all of the five Ks, but because they have not formally taken *amrit* they cannot be called Amritdhari Sikhs. All Amritdharis are Keshdharis, but only a small proportion of Keshdharis are Amritdharis.

Strictly speaking the Khalsa comprises only those who have taken initiation. In a narrow sense the Khalsa is, in other words, limited to Amritdhari Sikhs. They alone have formally promised to observe the Khalsa *Rahit*, with the five Ks at its centre, and for this reason they alone are members of the Khalsa which was established by Guru Gobind Singh. In common usage, however, the Khalsa is extended to cover Keshdhari Sikhs also. It is extended to all who observe the five Ks without necessarily being restricted to the Amritdhari Sikhs who have taken initiation.

Some Sikhs, it is true, hold that membership to the Khalsa is a privilege limited to Amritdharis and, as I have just acknowledged, their view is in a strict sense correct. The view expressed by common usage is, however, much more widely supported. This is held by both Amritdharis and Keshdharis, and regards the Khalsa as consisting of all those Sikhs who observe the five Ks. It comprises, in other words, all Keshdharis (some of whom are also Amritdharis) who maintain the five symbols. Those Sikhs who cut their hair are excluded.

Together the Amritdharis and Keshdharis (both men and women) form the Khalsa. Other people may belong to the Sikh Panth, but because they do not maintain these five symbols they do not belong to the Khalsa. They may be Sahajdharis, those who make no claim to Khalsa membership and who do not observe its *Rahit* (including the five Ks). Their number is now small, both in the Punjab and in other countries. Others will be members of families with Khalsa affiliations, but who have cut their hair. No name exists to describe these latter. In Western countries amongst migrant communities they are relatively common and are frequently mistaken as non-Sikh by Europeans and others.

'Orthodoxy' is very difficult to define satisfactorily. As we have seen, however, in the case of Sikhism non-Khalsa Sikhs provide us with a clear indication of its meaning. It is these non-Khalsa members of the Panth who are regarded as unorthodox, the term 'orthodox' being properly reserved for members of the Khalsa.

How then are non-Khalsa Sikhs regarded by members of the Khalsa?

Are they treated as members of the Panth or are they in effect excluded? Here one is confronted by the inevitable difference which in every religious faith the world over separates the liberal or lax from the rigorous or devout. The liberal among the Khalsa are prepared to accept the haircutting person who claims to be a Sikh, though they would not necessarily approve of the decision to forego the *Rahit*. The rigorous, on the other hand, are decidedly uneasy and in some cases will categorically refuse to accept the shaven or trimmed person as a Sikh.

A general rule is, however, accepted by most Khalsa Sikhs (whether generous or strict). The Khalsa represents the ideal mode and all are encouraged to adopt it. Others are tolerated as Sikhs, but it is only on the understanding that they are working their way towards full membership of the Khalsa. All the Panthic levers of power are in the hands of the Khalsa (at least in the Punjab homeland) and decisions concerning the Panth are usually taken with the situation of the Khalsa very much in the foreground. Pre-eminence within the Panth belongs unquestionably to the Khalsa and whilst others may be accepted as Sikhs their pattern of behaviour certainly meets with no approval.

Amritdhari and Keshdhari are accordingly both regarded as Khalsa Sikh (at least those Keshdhari who observe all five Ks and not just some of them). The Khalsa constitutes orthodox Sikhism and its members clearly dominate the social and political life of the Panth.

THE IMPORTANCE OF THE TURBAN TO MALE KHALSA SIKHS

Is the turban really so important to the Sikhs of the Khalsa? After all, it is not one of the five Ks. The turban may not appear in any text as one of the five Ks, but it is certainly declared frequently (and with emphasis) by Khalsa Sikhs as an essential addition to the male uniform. This surely is the inescapable fact about the turban. It is the crown of apparel for the Khalsa, regarded as absolutely essential for all adult males who are members. Their visible identity is expressed by it as much as by any of the five Ks.

The turban is regarded as desirable for a number of reasons. First, it is hygienic. Caps and hats are much more difficult to keep clean than the washing of all length of cotton fabric. Secondly, it is comfortable to wear in both hot weather and cold. In the heat the layer of hair conserves the coolness of the head, and the turban provides welcome protection in the cold. Thirdly, it provides greater protection for the head than a standard headgear. Fourthly, it is inexpensive to purchase and with a little practice it is simple to wind on the head. Fifthly, it is firmly anchored on the head and the wind does not blow it off. And sixthly, it is more suitable than the bare head when the wearer is handling food or other delicate items.

But these are merely reasons why the turban may be regarded as a suitable headgear. They are not sufficient to justify it as mandatory and many people (in India as well as in the rest of the world) manage quite satisfactorily without one. But then other people do not have to retain their hair uncut. This is the key issue. Khalsa Sikhs are required to retain uncut hair by their religious faith and this simple fact places them in an inescapably different position. For them (at least for the adult males) the turban is a neat and tidy means of covering the hair which (as we have been emphasizing) must be kept uncut. There is no other satisfactory form of covering the hair. One need only imagine uncovered hair to realize how superior the turban is as a means of containing and controlling hair which has to be tied on the head in a top-knot. The hair could in theory be allowed to hang loose. This, however, would be quite impractical. There are too many tasks which the male member of the Khalsa is required to perform which would be altogether impossible if the hair is not bound—tasks which will immediately occur to members of the Royal Canadian Maounted Police as they reflect on their various duties.

The turban is, therefore, of vital importance to the presentation of the male member of the Khalsa, significantly adding to the dignity of his appearance. Women are not normally required to wear one, though one variety of sectarian opinion does indeed require full-scale turbans for female members of the Khalsa as well as male. All orthodox Sikhs are, however, firm on the subject of turbans for male members of the Khalsa.

And indeed it goes even further than the argument based on appearance. For the orthodox Sikh the wearing of a turban is an essential part of being a Sikh. Because he is a member of the Khalsa adult male Sikh must wear a turban. For generations past, the turban has been compulsory for the male Khalsa and if he is to stand forth as an orthodox believer he must do so as the wearer of a turban. It is acknowledged that some members of the Panth do not wear them. As we have seen, however, they are not members of the Khalsa, nor would they be described as orthodox.

CONCLUSIONS

The orthodox Sikh community is the Khalsa and can be identified by some key doctrines which include adherence to the five Ks. One of these items consists of uncut hair (*kesh*). In order to cover his uncut hair neatly a turban is essential for a Khalsa Sikh male. The turban is seen as a sacred and absolutely vital symbol for the Sikh Khalsa.

NOTES

1. The Sikh Gurdwaras Act, 1925 (Punjab Act, No. VIII of 1925) as modified by the Government of India (Adaptation of Indian Laws) Order, 1937, and Punjab Act, No. VII of 1938, pp. 3-4. Since India became independent, the word 'State' has been substituted for 'Provincial'.

2. 'Guru' is expressed as a singular as all ten Gurus are believed to have embodied the one divine Spirit or 'eternal Guru'. The image commonly used is that of a single flame igniting ten torches in turn. On the death of the tenth Guru in 1708 the role or function of the Guru is believed to have passed to the sacred scripture which is known thereafter as the *Guru Granth Sahib*.

3. The first established arrival of Sikh settlers in Canada was in 1903 when ten men landed in Vancouver.

4. The proportion of Amritdhari Sikhs within the Panth is very roughly estimated at 15 per cent.

5. Sahajdhari Sikhs are mainly from urban castes (Khatris, Aroras and Ahluwalias).

Sikh *Kirpan* in California Schools

The Social Concerns of Symbols, the Cultural Politics of Identity and the Limits of Multiculturalism

VINAY LAL

In recent years, American courts, besides numerous government institutions and public bodies, have deliberated on what would appear to be a rather esoteric issue, but one which directly addresses the right to free exercise of religion guaranteed by the Bill of Rights and subsequent legislation. Across the state of California, certain children of the Sikh faith have been wearing to school, in accordance with the tenets of their faith, a small knife or dagger that the Sikhs describe as a *kirpan*. In January, 1994, three siblings, Rajinder, Sukhjinder, and Jaspreet Cheema, were observed to be wearing *kirpans* under their clothes while at school. They were suspended on the ground that a *kirpan* was to be construed as falling within the definition of a weapon offered in the California Penal and Education Codes and other regulations, which make it a criminal offence, subject to specified exceptions, to bring or possess specified weapons, including knives and daggers, upon the grounds of, or within, a public or private school. Subsequently, the Superintendent of the Livingston Union School District in Merced County, where the Cheema family has been residing for some years, was approached by the American Civil Liberties Union with a request that the School District reconsider its position, but the members of the Board refused to lift the ban on *kirpans* or to allow the Cheema children to attend school while the matter was under dispute. On 15 April 1994, the Cheema family filed suit and sought a preliminary and permanent injunction preventing the District from excluding Sikh students from attending school without violating their right to the free exercise of religion. Such an injunction was denied by the District Judge; the US Court of Appeals, Ninth Circuit, subsequently reversed and remanded the District Judge's decision. On remand, the District Judge ordered that the Cheema children be allowed to carry, subject to certain conditions, *kirpans* to school. However, matters were not to end there, as a Bill unanimously passed in the California Senate, that would have allowed Sikh children to carry *kirpans* to school on the ground that possession of such *kirpans* constituted an integral part of a recognized religious practice, was vetoed by Pete Wilson, Governor of California, who declared himself unable to 'abandon public safety to the resourcefulness of a thousand school districts'.[1]

As one of the first cases to be tried under the Religious Freedom Restoration Act (RFRA) of 1993, *Rajinder Singh Cheema et al., v. Harold V. Thompson et al.*, is a case of unusual legal importance. The provision in the Bill of Rights allowing for the free exercise of religion has been one of the most keenly contested aspects of American constitutional and political history, and the enactment by Congress of the Religious Freedom Restoration Act of 1993, which was struck down as unconstitutional by the Supreme Court in 1997, suggests that the duties of the state in matters pertaining to religion will continue to be a matter of controversy, subject to continuous (and conflicting) interpretation by the courts.

I propose, in the first instance, to sketch a history of the *kirpan*, and then to locate sociologically and historically the claims pursued by both parties to the conflict. I shall argue at some length that the politics of Sikhism in the diaspora cannot be divorced, as it was in the arguments of both the defence and the prosecution in the Cheema case, from the politics of Sikhism in the land of its birth. I shall then move to an exploration of the moral and political complexities of a problem where the religious convictions of a particular community, when their exercise has not shown to be detrimental to the rights of other members of society, are none the less posited against the consideration, preeminent as it must be for any state, of public safety. Finally, as I shall suggest, the complex legal arguments, establishing that the Livingston School District was not entitled to prevent the Cheemas from the free exercise of their religious convictions and obligations, are persuasive but our endorsement of the right to the free exercise of religion need not hinge upon an acceptance of the arguments presented by the plaintiffs' attorneys. It must be unequivocally clear that our acceptance of the right of the Cheemas, and thus of all Sikh children, to be in possession of *kirpans* while at school must be forthcoming even if the legal interpretation of the Religious Freedom Restoration Act does not support such a right, as the Supreme Court has now ruled.

While I am not yet prepared to advance, at least in the confines of this paper, an argument for an unconditional right to self-determination, or even an argument for some unadulterated and transcendent notion of 'rights', dominant communities must, it appears, learn to dispossess themselves of their privileges. Situations such as those in which the Cheema children found themselves, and in which thousand others are placed daily, provide the only test, not merely of a culture's capacity for resilience, but of its willingness to be chivalrous, its ability to live with some discomfort, its adherence to the ethos of cultural pluralism and accommodation, its celebration of the plurality of knowledge, and its readiness to create the conditions for the ecological survival of plurality.

I. THE *KIRPAN* AND THE FIVE SYMBOLS OF THE SIKH FAITH

The history of Sikhism is a subject which has been detailed in innumerable monographs and learned studies, and while this history need not detain us, certain elementary—though not always incontestable—statements of 'fact' need to be set out.[2] The Sikh religion was founded in India by Guru Nanak (1469-1539) nearly 500 years ago. Born in the Punjab, Nanak rebelled against the obscurantism and ritualism of Hinduism, and questioned the authority of India's sacerdotal caste, the Brahmans. Nanak preached a simple faith shorn of idolatry and predicated on the equality of all men. He perceived God as *sat*—epistemologically 'truth', ontologically 'being', the Supreme Reality, omnipotent and omniscient. An itinerant master of monotheism, Nanak roamed over the Punjab and gathered a number of disciples or *shishyas*, from which the word Sikh was ultimately derived. For Nanak they were neither Hindus nor Muslims, but when he died, adherents of both faiths laid claim to his remains. In the words of one couplet,

Guru Nanak, the King of Fakirs.
To the Hindu a Guru, to the Mussulman a Pir.[3]

Nanak chose as his successor Angad (1539-52), the second Guru of the Sikh faith, who was followed, in turn, by eight others. Angad developed the Gurmukhi script and collected the writings of Nanak. The fourth Guru, Ram Das (1574-81), founded the holy city of Amritsar, where his successor Arjan (1581-1606) built a gurdwara (literally, doorway to the Guru) or Sikh temple. Guru Arjan also engaged in the construction of numerous other gurdwaras, and gave definite shape to the compilation of Nanak's writings, which along with the hymns of Hindu and Muslim saints and the writings of the other Gurus were constituted into the *Adi Granth* or *Guru Granth Sahib*, the holy book of the Sikhs. The Sikhs thereby became, in the words of one scholar, a 'textual community'.[4] Guru Arjan's efforts to put his faith on a firm foundation and secure for it an organizational structure attracted the attention of India's Mughal dynasty, and he was consequently put to death in the city of Lahore. This was, on the conventional account, also the fate of Tegh Bahadur (1664-75), the ninth Guru, who refused conversion to Islam. His son, Gobind Singh (1675-1708), having assumed the leadership of his people at the age of ten, conceived of a plan in his later years to save the Sikh community from possible extinction and safeguard the interests of the community. He initiated five of his followers, known as the *Panj Piare*, or the Five Beloved, into a new brotherhood which he called the Khalsa, or the Pure ones.[5] They were given, as would have any monks joining a Hindu order, new names to each of which was attached the suffix 'Singh' or lion. (Sikh Khalsa women receive the name 'Kaur') They were also enjoined to wear, as a mark of their devotion to the faith and as an indication of their membership to the Khalsa, *Panj Kakar* or five symbols: *kesh* (uncut hair), *kangha* (a comb), *kara* (a steel bangle), *kirpan* (a sword or knife) and *kachha* (special breeches or undergarments). Having further commanded them to abstain from tobacco, alcohol, and *halal* meat (that is, meat slaughtered in the Muslim manner of slowly bleeding an animal to death), Gobind Singh then baptized the five men, and was in turn baptised by them. Thus was formed the Khalsa.

As every Sikh Khalsa male was henceforth to be known as a 'Singh' or lion, Gobind Singh in one stroke had not only signified his radical commitment to equality by the obliteration of the mark of caste identification,[6] but also prepared the Khalsa for a life of militant devotion to their faith. While the reasoning that prompted Gobind Singh to command the initiates into the Khalsa brotherhood to embrace the *Panj Kakar* is less certain, the scholar Jit Singh Uberoi has offered what is undoubtedly a compelling interpretation of the five symbols and their place within Sikhism. He has suggested that we view Guru Gobind Singh's injunctions in relation to certain rites of renunciation or sanyasa that were prevalent throughout the Punjab (and indeed the rest of India) in his time. In the initiation rites undertaken by the Hindu sanyasi, he would—having found a Guru—have his beard, moustache, and head entirely shaved. The neophyte of the jogi order, says Uberoi, 'is first made to fast for two or three days. A knife is then driven into the earth, and the candidate vows by it not to (1) engage in trade, (2) take employment, (3) keep dangerous weapons, (4) become angry when abused, and (5) marry.'[7] Such a life could only signify disinvestiture and renunciation, while Guru Gobind Singh, in requiring Sikh men to keep their hair long, clearly intended the Sikh initiation rite to be understood as an investiture and an act of affirmation, standing in antithesis to the rites of Hindu renunciation. The anti-depilatory taboo, argues Uberoi, is to be understood 'as a specific inversion in symbolic terms of the custom of total depilation' enjoined by sanyasis, jogis, and others, indeed as the 'permanent renunciation of renunciation', the 'negation of the negation.'[8] Uberoi's argument is complicated by the circumstance that in some Muslim and Hindu orders, the hair is worn long, but as he notes, it is then worn as matted hair, dressed in ashes. In the Sikh conception, the function of 'constraining the hair and imparting an orderly arrangement to it' falls upon the *kangha* (comb), and the *kesh* and *kangha* thus form a unitary and complementary pair. A similar complementary pair is formed by the *kirpan* (sword) and *kara* (steel bangle), and Uberoi suggests that 'the steel bracelet imparts the same orderly control over the sword which the comb does the hair'.[9]

Uberoi admits that 'the custom of wearing long and unshorn hair (*kesh*) is among the most cherished and distinctive signs of an individual's membership of the Sikh Panth, and it seems always to have been so'.[10] Long hair, because it is distinctive, particularly when it is rolled up in a turban, as it is among modern-day Sikhs, appears to be the most characteristic sign of a Khalsa Sikh male. A recent piece of legislation, the Delhi Gurdwara Act 82 of 1971, went so far as to define a Sikh as a 'person who professes the Sikh religion, believes and follows the teachings of *Sri Guru Granth Sahib* and the ten Gurus only *and keeps unshorn hair*'. If it had to be ascertained whether a person were a Sikh, the Act further states, the person in question would be required to make the following declaration: 'I solemnly affirm that I am a Keshdhari Sikh, that I believe in and follow the teachings of *Sri Guru Granth Sahib* and the ten Gurus only, and that I have no other religion.'[11] Keshdhari, or orthodox, Sikhs keep their hair long. However, as Uberoi argues, and as Sikh scholars would indebatably agree, despite the preeminence seemingly attached to *kesh* or unshorn hair the five symbols are of a piece, and together constitute 'the authenticating sign and seal of Śikhism'.[12] They were almost certainly seen as belonging together on the person of the Sikh, and in one of the earliest colonial accounts we have of the Sikhs, the Khalsa Sikhs were described thus: 'The disciples of Gobind were required to devote themselves to arms, always to have steel about them in some shape or other, to wear a blue dress, to allow their hair to grow, to exclaim when they met each other, *Waheguruji ka Khalsa! Waheguruji ki Fateh!*' ('The Khalsa are the chosen of God. Victory be to our God').[13] Indeed, colonial officials, who were predisposed towards viewing Sikhs as one of India's preeminent 'martial races', and saw in the support rendered to the British by the Sikhs during the difficult days of the Indian rebellion of 1857-8 the vindication of their views, considered the observance of the symbols among Sikhs as not only a true sign of their faith, but as conferring upon them the military prowess for which they were esteemed. 'The best practical test of a true Sikh,' wrote the author of a manual intended for army officials, 'is to ascertain whether calling himself a Sikh he wears uncut hair and abstains from smoking.'[14] Only those Sikhs who faithfully observed the Khalsa symbols were recruited into the army.

It is no surprise, then, that Sikh scholars are agreed that the five Ks 'are the symbol of Sikh solidarity, unity and strength'.[15] If Uberoi is right, more particularly, in suggesting that the *kirpan* should be viewed as being conjoined with the *kara*, then it follows that the *kirpan* is 'a sword ritually constrained and thus made into the mark of every citizen's honour, not only of the soldier's vocation'.[16] A sword that is 'ritually constrained' is a sword that is bound to do only the work of justice, to be drawn on behalf of the oppressed and the weak, to be offered only in defence. The sword can be employed only when all other avenues have been explored and exhausted, and indeed failure to do so at that time would be tantamount to complicity in acts of evil and oppression. Though the sword was the natural adornment of the soldier, Guru Gobind, in designating the *kirpan* as one of the five distinctive symbols of the Khalsa, was clearly intending to convey that the men of the Khalsa would be much like soldiers in displaying bravery and fearlessness, but as their sword was to be the sword of baptism, they were also to exercise restraint. It is with the sword that the Guru baptized the first five initiates. As the story goes, the Guru asked for five men who would be willing to give their heads; eventually one man stepped forth and was taken into a tent, from which the Guru emerged with a blood-stained sword; and, then, another four men volunteered (no doubt with great hesitation and even trepidation), all seemingly dispatched in the same manner. But the Guru then emerged from the tent with the five men and five decapitated goats.

Guru Gobind's father, let us also recall, had been martyred, and the fear of persecution had led other Sikhs to lead lives of anonymity. While Guru Gobind was unwilling to let his people be martyred by Muslim rulers, he did not think that they were to evade persecution by merging into the crowd. Thus the sword, becoming a characteristic mark of the Sikhs, was to render them intrepid, willing to forgo their lives of fear and anonymity for recognition by others, and place them on the path of self-recognition. As an eighteenth-century writer, Ratan Singh Bhangu, was to claim,

the Guru reasoned and from thought he proceeded to action. His followers were to emerge as splendid warriors, their uncut hair bound in turbans; and as warriors all were to bear the name 'Singh'. This, the Guru knew, would be effective. He devised a form of baptism administered with the sword, one which would create a Khalsa staunch and unyielding. His followers would destroy the empire, each Sikh horseman believing himself to be a king. All weakness would be beaten out of them and each, having taken the baptism of the sword, would thereafter be firmly attached to the sword.[17]

As I have suggested, the attachment to the sword, or the *kirpan*, must be perceived as an attachment to an 'object' that becomes an inalienable part of oneself, constitutive of a life of affirmation, honour, and self-respect; and to forgo the *kirpan*, at least on the orthodox view, is to relinquish one's identity as a Sikh observant of the faith.[18]

II. THE REACH OF THE *KIRPAN*

Political Constructions of a Sacred Symbol

Though the story of the *kirpan*, from the time of Guru Gobind Singh's death to the early part of the twentieth century, when the *kirpan* must have first surfaced in North America, obviously does not belong within the confines of this paper, a few remarks about the manner in which various Governments of India in the twentieth century have sought to constrain, as it were, the reach of the *kirpan* will contribute to an understanding of the contours of the present debate. By the late nineteenth century, Harjot Oberoi has argued, the Singh Sabhas or Sikh Associations had systematized the strict adherence to the five Ks, along with other observances (such as visits to Sikh shrines and abstention from prohibited foods), as constitutive of a true and unambiguous Sikh identity.[19] *Kirpans* were to become quite visible in the 1920s, which is often described as the first phase of militant Sikh participation in the nationalist movement. The Central Sikh League had been inaugurated on 30 December 1919; by the following summer, a number of District Sikh Leagues had been set up. It is around this time, as one historian has written, that 'the widespread adoption of Khalsa symbols denoting solidarity and militancy in the name of the faith' began to be observed. 'Sikhs began in increasing numbers to wear black turbans (a symbol of militancy) and *kirpans*.'[20] An agitation for the control of Sikh shrines that had first started in 1914, and had during the war been relegated to the background, was once again revived, and in this the Akalis, a group that ascribed its origins to Guru Gobind Singh, were to play a large role.

These Akalis, 'carrying large *kirpans*', also began to appear in public places during the summer of 1920.[21] The army was not spared of dissent either, and this was no small matter, as the Sikhs constituted a formidable presence in the army, out of all proportion to their share of the population. As the Punjab Government was to report in May 1920, 'A young sepoy of the Depot of the 34th Pioneers at Sialkot appeared on parade with a large *kirpan*, which he refused on religious grounds to give up. He was sentenced by court martial to one year imprisonment for insubordination. . . . The Sikh League are interesting themselves in the case.'[22]

While the movement for the 'liberation' of gurdwaras, whose administration was in the hands of priests (*mahants*) who were considered to be excessively 'Hinduized' and sometimes even pawns of the British, was to gain momentum, the Government of the Punjàb struggled to arrive at some policy which would enable them to prevent the public display of *kirpans*, and thus preserve their authority, without generating allegations of religious interference. It was clear that matters had come to a head: in December 1920, for example, Sikhs belonging to the newly constituted Shiromani Gurdwara Prabandhak Committee (SGPC), an organization committed to handing over management of the gurdwaras to true and strict followers of the faith, had forcibly occupied three gurdwaras, in each instance brandishing *kirpans* and axes. On numerous other occasions in 1921, Akalis 'armed with axes and *kirpan*' captured Sikh shrines; and in a government report on the agitation published in 1922, reference was specifically made to the *kirpan* as a 'Sikh religious emblem' that had 'figured so prominently in Sikh agitation during the past few years'. Less benignly, the author of the report noted that the 'lethal nature of this weapon, which has grown in size until it is now indistinguishable from a sword', had occasioned complaints from other Indian communities who desired to know why the Sikhs were being granted special privileges.[23]

By February 1922, the decision had been taken by the Punjab Government that district officers were to disarm Akali militants. For fear of offending the religious sensibilities of Sikhs, the Akalis were not to be divested of their *kirpans*, though the government sought to curtail their length. However, the SGPC was opposed to any such measure, as the Sikh faith imposes no limits on the size of the *kirpan*, and as though to underscore the sensitivity of the issue, a Sikh in one regiment went on a hunger strike on 7 February when he was forbidden from wearing a *kirpan* of a size larger than allowed by the regulations.[24] The SGPC agreed only that the misuse of the *kirpan* would entitle the government to take action, and it called upon the Sikhs in the army to observe regulations pertaining to the wearing of *kirpans* and black turbans.[25] The army staff, none the less, continued to maintain that the length of the *kirpan* be restricted to 9 inches, and it is at the behest of the army that the Government of India wrote to the Punjab Government to express its disapproval of the policy followed in the Punjab. The Government of India, wrote one official, had acquiesced in the view that it was not opportune to enforce limitations on the size of the *kirpans* when negotiations between the Punjab Government and SGPC on the questions of gurdwara management appeared to be making good progress. 'They are not, however,' he added, 'clear as to the reasons which have led the local government to authorize the wearing of swords and of *kirpans* indistinguishable from swords by Sikhs.' Though the Government of India recognized the wisdom of not instituting prosecutions, it thought that the Punjab Government had practically authorized, 'even though subject to conditions, the carrying of weapons prohibited by law'. The government of India could not see how *kirpans* 'practically indistinguishable from swords' were being 'worn with impunity', and noted that the 'question of imposing a definite limitation on the size of *kirpans* may require to be considered'.[26]

The question of what to do with *kirpans*, however, was sidelined for the moment, and with the passage of the Sikh Gurdwaras Act of 1925 the grievances of the SGPC and Khalsa Sikhs appear to have been partially resolved. Indeed, between 1925 and 1928, most of the provinces had passed legislation exempting Sikhs carrying *kirpans* from the provisions of the Indian Arms Act of 1878, which expressly forbid Indians from bearing arms.[27] Subsequent to the independence of India in 1947, the Sikhs were able to attain a further concession. Article 25 of the Constitution of India (1950), relating to the free exercise of religion, also stated in its explanatory clause that the wearing and carrying of *kirpans* was to be considered as being 'included in the profession of the Sikh religion'.[28] This meant that Sikhs throughout India could now carry *kirpans* of unspecified length in public without having contravened the law; the Constitution also appeared to be conceding that Sikh identity is distinct, as Sikhs alone were allowed the privilege of carrying *kirpans*. The second 'Explanation' following the Article, however, stipulated that references to Hindus and to Hindu religious institutions were to be so construed as to include adherents of Sikhism, Buddhism, and Jainism.[29] If Sikh identity was being affirmed in the first explanatory clause, the second clause appeared to assimilate Sikhs into the Hindu fold. Such a provision was always liable to become the basis for an allegation that an attempt was being made to eliminate Sikhs, render Sikhism sterile and even effeminate, or that in Hindu India Sikhs were bound to be a repressed minority.

At a conference of the Akali Dal, the political party representing the interest of the Khalsa Sikhs if not of the entire Panth, held in February 1981, Harcharan Singh Longowal, the president of the conference, reminded the gathering that the 'Sikh nation is unique in refusing to be absorbed in the Brahmanical traditions and modes of the Hindu nation' and that 'Sikhs were still struggling for asserting our rightful claim to our identity and nationhood'.[30] He also declared his intent to have certain demands, endorsed by the SGPC and forty-five in number, accepted by the Government of India, and to this end negotiations between the SGPC and the government began later in the year. Among these demands, which complained of the government's refusal to grant 'holy city' status to Amritsar, its failure to name any train the Golden Temple Express (after the Golden Temple in Amritsar), and of its negligence in safeguarding the life and property of Sikhs throughout India and abroad, was the demand that Sikhs be allowed to carry the *kirpan* aboard civilian aircraft on domestic and international flights.[31] This demand surfaced in many speeches by Sikh leaders, and it is reported that Jarnail Singh Bhindranwale, the leader of the violent secessionist movement, urged his followers to carry the *kirpan* aboard Indian Airlines and Air India flights with the following words: 'If a Hindu can wear his sacred thread (*janeu*) which is his sign, why can't a Sikh carry his sword?'[32]

Certain demands were conceded, including the right of Sikhs to carry *kirpans* of stipulated length on domestic flights,[33] but some substantial differences remained. Disaffection among militant Sikhs continued to spread, and the story of the bloody aftermath—including a campaign of terror and assassination in which many Sikhs and Hindus were the victims, the gross violation of the rights of many Sikhs to their life and livelihood by Indian police and armed forces in their drive to eliminate the terrorists, the fortification of the Golden Temple by Sikh terrorists led by Bhindranwale, the storming of the Golden Temple by the Indian Army, the death of Indira Gandhi at the hand of two Sikh assassins, the carnage unleashed upon Sikhs in Delhi, and the continuing war of terror and secession before the eventul 'pacification' of militant Sikhs a few years ago—has been told in numerous works.[34] But what is most pertinent is that, particularly during the spread of Sikh militancy under Bhindranwale's leadership, Sikhs themselves were prominent if not preeminent among the victims of Bhindranwale's campaign to eliminate his enemies. As Rajiv Kapur has so succinctly stated, Bhindranwale had emerged, from the outset of his new responsibilities as the head of a small center of Sikh religious learning, 'as a rigid champion of Sikh orthodoxy. He toured Sikh villages, exhorted his congregation not to discard Khalsa symbols and baptized hundreds. An essential feature of his preaching was that, in keeping with Sikh traditions, all Sikhs should bear weapons.'[35] Bhindranwale urged his audience with the exhortation *'shastradhari howo'*, that is to become the bearers of weapons, and as Veena Das has so aptly noted, the 'most visible sign of the masculinity of the Sikh in this discourse is his sword'. There was nothing that Bhindranwale more ardently desired than that Sikhs 'shed their femininity', and this was to be achieved not only by wielding the sword, but by emphatically repudiating Hinduism, construed as a feminine faith. Bhindranwale was to propound the idea that Sikhs had been a 'race whose history is written in the blood of martyrs', and such a race of men could not conceivably be deemed to have accepted the designation of Mahatma Gandhi as the 'father of the nation', whose very techniques of resistance were feminine. 'Can those who are the sons of the valiant guru, whose symbol is the sword,' Bhindranwale was to ask his audience, 'ever accept a woman like [the] Mahatma as their father?'[36]

Bhindranwale and his followers targeted not merely those Sikh leaders who were opposed to his teachings, and such newspaper editors as had dared to raise their voices against him, but 'moderate' Sikhs as well who had abandoned the symbols of their faith and thus relapsed into Hinduism, abjuring their masculinity for a contemptible femininity, renouncing (as the militants imagined) the strict tenets of their pure faith for the idolatry and softness of a pluralistic Sikhism quite comfortable with, if not indistinguishable from, Hinduism. This is the old fear that haunts every Sikh who is keen on maintaining boundaries that constantly invite transgression. Perhaps these symbols alone remained, nearly five hundred years after the birth of the faith, to differentiate Sikhs from Hindus—itself a rather desperate thought; and if these too, perchance, were not observed, then who could say who is a Sikh? As if in grim testimony of Bhindranwale's premonitions about the frail nature of Sikh identity, many Sikhs attempted to escape the holocaust unleashed upon them following the assassination of Indira Gandhi by shaving their beard and cutting short their hair; others, not so lucky, were first shaved before being burnt alive by the paid hooligans of party and local bosses.[37]

III. INALIENABLE SYMBOLS IN AN ALIEN LAND?

The Controversy over Kirpans in California Schools

Conflicts that rage within a country are often echoed within the lives of emigrants settled abroad. The movement among Bhindranwale and other extremists, many of whom are no longer living, for a separate state called Khalistan was to receive substantial support from Sikhs settled overseas. Jagjit Singh Chauhan, an advocate of armed violence against the Indian state, set up a sovereign state of Khalistan from his base in London, and became its self-styled President. With the support of other wealthy or influential Sikhs, such as the Californian Didar Singh Bains, who is reputed to be the world's biggest peach farmer, Chauhan canvassed among the substantial populations of Sikhs in the US, Britain, Canada, and (the former) West Germany for support. The All-India Sikh Students' Federation, the militant youth wing of the Akali Dal, established chapters in the US, Canada, and Britain, and branches of the Dal Khalsa, set up in India in 1978 'with the avowed object of demanding the creation of an idependent sovereign Sikh State', were opened in Britain and West Germany in 1983.[38] The attack upon the Golden Temple, and the brutal violence unleashed upon Sikhs following the assassination of Indira Gandhi, were bound to embitter some Sikhs overseas. 'Many Sikhs in Yuba City,' writes Bruce La Brack in his recent study of Sikhs in California, 'and elsewhere outside of South Asia have now embraced the idea of Khalistan as the *only* alternative to the present impasse and are willing to support it ideologically and financially.'[39] His study does not indicate the dissensions among Sikhs overseas, and this is a matter to which I shall have occasion to return. There has also been, in the matter of Sikh children carrying *kirpans* to schools, disagreements among the Sikh community, and this too is a matter I shall leave for later.

Bruce La Brack further notes that the symbols of the faith were not strictly observed by Sikhs, if indeed at all, during the period from around 1900-10, when the Sikh presence first became noticeable on the West Coast of the United States and Canada, to nearly the late 1950s. The Stockton Gurdwara, for example, even allowed worshippers to enter the shrine with their shoes on and without requiring them to cover their heads.[40] But with the arrival of students and other new emigrants in the 1950s, and 'a reawakening of concern for tradition in older resident Sikhs', 'the wearing of the five Ks seems to have gained· some acceptance'. Though some newcomers were 'persuaded to shave in conformity to what older Sikhs felt were American standards of dress and grooming', the 'Sikh newcomers generally retained the beard and turban'. A few of the older Sikhs themselves re-adopted the symbols of the faith; and La Brack concludes from this that 'external orthodoxy was increasing'.[41] La Brack makes no mention of the *kirpan*. He also suggests, rather unpersuasively, that the substance of the debate over why some Sikhs re-adopted the five symbols is 'not as important as . . . its presence'.[42] Could it perhaps be the case that in the first few decades, when discrimination against Asians was rampant, and Sikhs were in any case assimilated into the 'Hindu' fold, that Sikhs wisely wished to draw no further attention to themselves?[43] In the Punjab itself, during the 1950s, there was a movement for a Punjabi Suba or Punjabi homeland, and there can be little doubt that the self-assurance of Sikhs overseas received a boost from the events back in India. Moreover, by the late 1950s and early 1960s, the Sikhs in California had made a considerable presence for themselves, and some had reached positions of enormous affluence. The time was certainly ripe for asserting the faith; and along with unshorn hair, there is no more moving and visible symbol of the faith than the *kirpan*.

The acceptance of the *kirpan*, however, has been fraught with difficulties, and there has been a flurry of political and legal activity over the last few years, culminating in the legal decision in the Cheema case, and the aborted attempt by the California Assembly to enact legislation that would permit Sikh children to carry *kirpans* to schools without the fear of inviting official sanctions. To recapitulate the circumstances of the Cheema case, three children of the Cheema family residing near Merced, California, in the Livingston Union School District, were baptized as Khalsa Sikhs during the school recess in December 1993. When school reconvened in January, they returned wearing the five symbols of their faith, including the *kirpan*. The *kirpans* were worn under their clothes, as is common in the case of baptized Sikhs at work or school, and were thus not openly visible to others. One of the three children was, however, observed to be wearing a *kirpan* by his classmate, and the matter having been brought to the attention of the school principal, the Cheema children were at once suspended from school. It was explained that, in having brought *kirpans* to school, the children had contravened District regulations as well as the California Penal Code, Section 626.10 of which makes it a public offense to bring to school, with specified exemptions, any 'dirk, dagger, ice pick, knife having a blade longer than 2.5 inches', as well as numerous other specified objects.[44] The *kirpan*, the Cheema family were told, was to be considered a weapon within the meaning of the existing legislation. When the District refused to reconsider lifting the ban it had imposed upon the Cheema children unless they were willing to leave their *kirpans* at home, the American Civil Liberties Union asked the District for a reconsideration of its position, pointing out that in another School District the matter had been resolved 'in a manner which preserved the rights of Sikhs to attend school while wearing their *kirpans*'. A meeting of the School Board was then convened, though as attorneys for the Cheemas were to point out, members of the Board received a Memorandum from the Superintendent's office in which they were advised to adhere to the policy of 'no knives in school' in the light of the school's 'compelling interest' in furnishing 'an environment which is perceived to be safe'. It was proposed, as a 'viable alternative', to allow the children to wear a 'symbolic necklace replica' of a *kirpan*, though why the wearing of such a replica should have required the permission of school authorities remains a mystery. In the event, the Board refused to entertain the position taken by the Cheema family, and indeed the Sikh adults who had come to this public meeting were themselves threatened with arrest for having arrived at the meeting while wearing their own *kirpans*. The District was once again requested 'to at least allow the Cheema children to return to school while the legality of defendants' actions was being litigated', but this request was also rejected. The District Court was then moved by the counsel for the Cheema family, Stephen Bomse and the ACLU, to issue an injunction preventing the School District from excluding Sikh students from attending school without violating their right to the free exercise of religion under the Religious Freedom Restoration Act of 1993. The District Judge, Garland Burrell, Jr., refused to issue such an injunction, but on appeal, The Court of Appeals for the Ninth Circuit reversed and remanded the District Court's decision.[45]

In considering the case presented by the plaintiffs in the Court of Appeals, a number of considerations come to the fore. First, as the plaintiffs argued, similar cases had arisen in other School Districts, in the United States as well as Canada, which has a very substantial Sikh population, where Khalsa Sikh students had been allowed to attend school while wearing *kirpans*. They noted that Sikh students in the Selma Unified School District had expressly been allowed to carry *kirpans*, and the Superintendent of Schools had stated: 'I am unaware of any actual or threatened incidents of *kirpan*-related violence or other form of *kirpan* misuse, in this District or elsewhere' (BOA, 9). The official placed in charge of multicultural education in the Surrey School District in British Columbia had stated that schools in her district had 'several thousand Sikh students', 'many' of whom 'attend wearing *kirpans*' without any problem. As she emphasized in a letter attached to her declaration in February 1994, 'since the beginning of this century, baptized Sikhs have been attending public schools wearing *kirpans*. In this long period of time, there is no record of an association between *kirpans* and violence, and there is no record of *kirpans* being used inappropriately' (BOA, 10). The plaintiffs also argued that in Ontario, the Court ordered the School District to admit Sikh children wearing *kirpans*, as a study had shown that most other School Districts in Canada follow a similar policy; and indeed the Court went so far as to state that 'there is no evidence that *kirpans* have sparked a violent incident in any school, no evidence that any other School Board in Canada bars *kirpans*, and no evidence of a student anywhere in Canada using a *kirpan* as a weapon' (BOA, 11). A similar study in Calgary, commissioned by the School Board, not only recommended that the School District 'recognize the right of Khalsa Sikhs to wear *kirpans*', it noted that in numerous districts Sikh children wearing *kirpans* had been accommodated without the necessity of having to institute a policy (BOA, 11).

The plaintiffs had, then, established that throughout California and Canada, other School Districts had been able to accommodate the religious beliefs and practices of Khalsa Sikhs without compromising the safety of other school children and they had, secondly, brought to the Court's attention the inability of the Livingston School District to furnish a single instance of violence in schools, either in its own district or for that matter anywhere else, in which the *kirpan* had been used.[46] The plaintiffs then proceeded to provide further grounds for why an exemption ought to have been granted to Sikh children. Although the school authorities were inclined to view the *kirpan* as little better than a weapon, they had ignored the fact that the Cheema children, much like other baptized Sikhs, had been required to undergo 'an intensive training course to become familiar with the obligations of the Khalsa'. If they were required to wear the five Ks at all times, even while bathing and sleeping, they were also advised that the *kirpan* was not to be used as a weapon, and was to be removed from its sheath only for certain religious observances, certainly never as an offensive weapon to harm others; and the initiates were also 'required to affirm their understanding of, and commitment to, these principles as a condition of initiation' (BOA, 6-7). One 'expert' in the Sikh religion had stated in his declaration that 'every Khalsa Sikh is carefully schooled in the obligations concerning the *kirpan* just as they are schooled in their other religious duties' (BOA, 11-12).

Perhaps more significantly, the School District had a mistaken conception of the nature of its duty to provide, equally to all children, an environment that was safe and conducive to learning. School Boards had undoubtedly to set reasonable guidelines to ensure safety, but as the study commissioned in Calgary had concluded, a School District 'is not expected to guarantee the absolute safety of students for of course this is impossible. Many items common and necessary to an educational setting can be used to inflict harm or damage if the will is there' (BOA, 11). If a weapon were to be construed merely as any object with the capacity of inflicting harm, then it stood to reason that such objects as are commonly allowed in schools—scissors, compasses, baseball bats—and which clearly can be used as offensive weapons ought not to be so allowed. While guns and brass knuckles on the one hand, and acid in the laboratory and bread knives in the cafeteria on the other hand, are all material things that might be used to inflict harm, the latter objects are allowed because they fulfil a necessary and legitimate function. *Kirpans* were to be construed as falling within the latter category: as religious symbols, they are indispensable to the life of Khalsa Sikhs (BOA, 22-4). Moreover, whatever theoretical danger the *kirpan* posed, the risk had been further minimized by the concessions already agreed to by the Cheema family. While the blade length of 3 inches exceeded the legally permitted length of 2.5 inches, the *kirpan* was much duller than a typical knife, and the family had agreed to having the *kirpans* sowed down 'so tightly that even the adult members of the Livingston School board were unable to remove the *kirpan* from its sheath' (BOA, 25).[47]

Two conclusions followed. The obligation of the school was only to provide all children with a safe environment, but in choosing to exclude Khalsa Sikh children carrying *kirpans*, the School District was seeking to turn the school into a 'hermetically sealed' environment (BOA, 24). This is neither possible nor even reasonable. As the attorneys of the plaintiffs noted, even a child's home is only a 'reasonably, not a perfectly, safe world'. Parents often keep loaded guns in their home, for instance, 'although we know to a certainty that some children accidentally will be injured or killed as a result' (BOA, 24). We do not, however, altogether ban guns. The District Court, submitted the plaintiffs, had additionally erred in referring to the *kirpan*'s 'inalienable' character as a 'knife'. The *kirpan*'s 'inalienable' character, quite to the contrary, 'is as a sacred symbol in the Sikh religion', and the fact that the *kirpan* could, in theory, be used to inflict injury did not alter its 'inalienable' nature as a religious emblem. A baseball bat might well be construed as a piece of wood, or an object for hammering in a nail into a piece of wood, but preeminently it remains a special kind of sporting implement used to hit a round ball. It can no doubt be used, and indeed it has been so used, to smash a person's skull, or inflict some other grievous wound, but that does not alter its fundamental characteristic as a 'baseball bat'. Similarly, the essential characteristic of a *kirpan* is that it is a religious symbol of the faith: that is indeed its ontological status, and to construe it as a weapon is to do the *kirpan* injustice, to commit an act of epistemic violence, to surreptitiously plunge the sword into the backbone of the faith.

The District, then, had failed to show that the Livingston School District is in some manner unique, and that the experiences of School Districts elsewhere cannot serve as a guide to the school authorities. The District had likewise failed to establish that there had been previously any difficulty in allowing Sikh children to wear *kirpans* at school, and that something in the history of the School District, or indeed in the history of the Sikhs and their religion, warranted the belief that a *kirpan* represents a real threat as an object of violence. Nor had the District established that the *kirpan* has ever been employed as an offensive (or for that matter defensive) 'weapon' in schools. Did 'fear and discomfort' furnish adequate grounds for the argument that the state had a compelling interest in preventing the Cheema children from attending school; and if 'fear and discomfort' are to satisfy the compelling interest standard, is there any 'rational or evidentiary response' that could overcome such a defense (BOA, 21)? It 'is fair to question', noted the plaintiffs, 'whether the District's policy is rooted as much in a concern for school safety as in hostility to its small Sikh minority' (BOA, 26).

IV. LEGAL PLURALISM IN A MULTICULTURAL SOCIETY

In arguing their case on behalf of the Cheema family before the Court of Appeals, the attorneys for the plaintiffs and the American Civil Liberties Union had resorted to the recently enacted Religious Freedom Restoration Act (RFRA) of 1993.[48] Justifying the introduction of this legislation, Congress noted that the framers of the Constitution had clearly intended to secure 'the free exercise of religion as an unalienable right', and that the 'establishment clause' clearly prohibited the state from engaging in any activity leading to the establishment of any religion. If the state was bound to observe neutrality in matters pertaining to religion, it was also bound to recognize that 'laws "neutral" toward religion may burden religious exercise as surely as laws intended to interfere with religious exercise' (Sec. 2.a.2). Where such neutrality appeared to hinder the free exercise of religious thought, the state was bound to show that it had 'compelling justification' in refusing to grant an exemption from a certain law or regulation, and that the application of the burden of not granting an exemption 'is the least restrictive means of furthering that compelling governmental interest' (Sec. 2.a.3; Sec. 3.b.1-2). In refusing to grant an exemption to its policy of prohibiting weapons from school grounds in order to accommodate the right to free exercise of religion of its Khalsa Sikh students, the state had perforce to demonstrate that it had a compelling interest in so refusing an exemption, and that the course pursued of banning the children from school was the 'least restrictive means of furthering that compelling governmental interest'.

The Religious Freedom Restoration Act (RFRA), as the Congress itself had determined, became necessary because the 'compelling interest' standard had been massively weakened and compromised as a consequence of the Supreme Court's decision in the case of *Employment Division v. Smith*, 494 U.S. 872 (1990).[49] While a general consideration of this standard is well outside the parameters of this paper, it suffices to note that there are two broad versions of the right to the free exercise of religion. On the narrower view, 'religious liberty consists of not being discriminated against', and 'the law that applies to any religious minority will be the same as the law that applies to anybody else'.[50] Religious freedom consists in the right to equality. The less restrictive view is not merely a right to non-discrimination; it is a 'liberty right', a 'substantive right not to be regulated with respect to certain matters that are very important to the individual'. In the less restrictive view, the right to free exercise of religion is 'a right presumptively not to be regulated: the state should not burden a religious practice without a compelling reason'.[51]

It was the less restrictive view of RFRA, which obligated the state to provide a compelling reason to prevent someone from the free exercise of religion, which ACLU and the attorneys for the Cheema family invoked to have their position vindicated. In the Santeria animal sacrifice case,[52] where the City of Hialeah (Florida) had sought to curtail the free exercise of religion—and in particular the sacrifice of chickens—by adherents of the old African faith of Santeria, on the grounds that the state had a compelling interest to prevent injury to animals, harm to children, infringement of zoning regulations, and unsanitary conditions, the Supreme Court made it known that the compelling interest standard was not to be 'watered down'.[53] It was the more stringent standard, restored by the Supreme Court in the Santeria case, that Congress sought to give effect to through RFRA, and it was the standards stipulated by RFRA that the attorneys for the

Cheema family sought to have applied by the Court of Appeals in their case. The plaintiffs had, then, to show that they had a sincere religious belief; secondly, they had to establish that some government action substantially burdened or threatened the free exercise of their religion. Finally, provided the first two conditions were met, it was incumbent upon the government to show that its action in preventing the children of the Cheema family from attending school was 'in furtherance of a compelling governmental interest' and represented 'the least restrictive means of furthering that compelling . . . interest' (BOA, 18).

There was never any question that the Sikhs have a sincere religious belief. On the second issue, the District Court, while eventually refusing to issue an injunction that would have prevented the School District from excluding the Cheema children from their school, none the less conceded that '[a]s a result of the District's no-knives policy, Plaintiffs must choose either to follow a fundamental precept of their religion and forfeit the opportunity of attending school, or forsake one of the precepts of their faith in order to attend school' (BOA, 10n.13). Such a choice, the Court admitted, 'effectively penalizes the free exercise of [their] constitutional liberties', and 'this penalty constitutes a substantial burden on Plaintiffs' free exercise of their religion' (BOA, 10n.13). On the District Court's own ruling, then, it only remained to determine whether the School District had a compelling interest in ensuring the safety of all children attending the school where the Cheema children were enrolled, and whether the least restrictive means of ensuring such safety was to bar the Cheema children from attending school until such time as they were willing to keep their *kirpans* at home.

As we have seen, while the ACLU and the plaintiffs or the Cheema family were not unmindful of the fact that the school authorities are bound to provide an environment that is safe and conducive to learning, they did not think that any environment can be hermetically sealed. While the plaintiffs' attorneys did not state so, it is apparent that they thought that the School District was bound only to fulfil its obligation to an extent that can be considered reasonable; more pertinently, they were inclined to argue, *the question is not whether the school authorities had a compelling interest in maintaining a safe environment, as this is scarcely to be doubted, but whether they had a compelling interest in denying an exemption to its policy of 'no knives' in order to accommodate the free exercise rights of Khalsa Sikh children.* In the famous case of *Wisconsin* v. *Yoder,*[54] noted the plaintiffs' attorneys, the Supreme Court had ruled that Wisconsin's compelling interest in ensuring compliance with its system of compulsory school education, while valid in the generality of cases, was not such that Wisconsin could not deny an exemption to Amish children whose parents, for religious reasons, could not keep their children in schools beyond the eighth grade (BOA, 20). If the school could not provide an exemption, was it not bound to show that there were legitimate grounds for believing that the *kirpans* would be used to commit an act of violence on school grounds? The Livingston School District, as the plaintiffs' attorneys argued, had failed to provide any instance of an act of violence having been so committed, and it had just as evidently failed to consider that other School Districts had successfully accommodated Khalsa Sikh children who wished to carry their *kirpans* to school alongside their obligation to provide a safe environment conducive to the educational process. The school authorities had evidently also failed to meet the test that their purported 'compelling interest' could not be satisfied in a less restrictive fashion.

The failure of the Livingston School District to consider an exemption to its policy prohibiting knives and other weapons from school was rooted, submitted the plaintiffs' attorneys, in nothing but fear. But even the Supreme Court has ruled that fear cannot serve as the substantive basis for denying exemptions to policies or regulations that are otherwise justifiable: if fears are not always groundless, they are not always well-grounded either, and it is questionable whether apprehension of risk or danger, particularly in a case where all the evidence points to the absence of such danger, can be allowed to serve as the basis for certain policies that stand in opposition to fundamental rights guaranteed by the Constitution itself. Integration of neighbourhoods and schools might never have been possible if the authorities had allowed themselves to be paralysed by the fear of reprisals from white segregationists; and if authorities had succumbed to the 'near-hysteria' displayed by parents and School Boards, children diagnosed with HIV (and, in fewer cases, AIDS itself) would have been disallowed from schools when there was no evidence to suggest that there was legitimate cause for concern (BOA, 27-8). In one AIDS-related case,[55] a court in Florida, while recognizing the 'concern and fear . . . flowing from' the community, 'particularly from the parents of school age children', had unequivocally stated that 'the Court *may not* be guided by such community fear, parental pressure and the possibility of lawsuits. These obstacles, real as they may be, cannot be allowed to vitiate the rights [of the excluded students]. . .' (BOA, 28; emphasis in original). Pressing their case further, attorneys for the plaintiffs suggested that fear 'can mask the basest forms of prejudice', and that the argument from fear requires no evidence. What can the protection of first amendment rights mean when only the exercise of such rights as do not evoke someone's fear is allowed? 'Freedoms that are protected only when there is no cost or risk to others', the Court of Appeals was reminded, 'are scarcely freedoms at all' (BOA, 26).

V. CULTURAL PLURALISM AND THE POLITICS OF SOCIAL DIVERSITY

The Court of Appeals, as I have mentioned earlier, reversed and remanded the District Court's judgment. In ruling on a preliminary injunction, denied by the District Court, which would have barred the School District from applying its no-knives policy to ban the possessions of *kirpans* at school, the Court of Appeals stated: 'we weigh the likelihood of harm against the likelihood of success on the merits'. The Court of Appeals noted that the school had made no offer of accommodation; nor had it shown that banning the children from school was the 'least restrictive means of furthering [its] compelling governmental interest'. The Court of Appeals did not think that the District Court's view that some children might be frightened by the *kirpans*, or that others might think it unfair that some children were allowed knives while they were not, was anything more than 'speculation'. 'The district's concern that it treat all children the same is not a compelling interest,' the court stated, 'because accommodation sometimes requires exactly the opposite: accepting those who are different and recognizing that "fairness" does not always mean everybody must be treated identically.'[56] The District Court was thus enjoined to direct the parties to submit to 'an agreed plan of accommodation, which will protect the safety of the students and accommodate the religious requirements of the Cheema children'.[57] Following an impasse, the District Court ordered that the Cheema children were to be permitted to return to school with their *kirpans*, subject to certain conditions.[58]

Meanwhile, while the Court of Appeals was deliberating over the issue, a bill was pending before the California legislature to amend the California Penal Code (Sec. 626.20), which bans weapons from school grounds, to exempt the carrying of a knife as part of any recognized religious practice.[59] On 24 August 1994, the Assembly voted 44-22, over objections by Republicans (many of whom are members of the notorious National Rifle Association), to allow Sikh children to carry *kirpans* to school; and later in the month, the Senate passed the bill on a unanimous 30-0 vote.[60] This bill did not, however, receive the assent of the Governor of California: in his veto message, Pete Wilson, while admitting that the Bill addressed a 'venerable religious practice', and that the Sikhs had 'an exceptional record as law-abiding citizens', stated that he could not be a party to a piece of legislation which 'authorize[s] the carrying of knives on school grounds' and which would mean abandoning 'public safety to the resourcefulness of a thousand school districts'.[61] It is not unpredictable that Wilson, who has scarcely compiled a flattering record for protection of minority rights, should have vetoed the bill. The veto does not preclude School Districts, acting on their own discretion, from granting exemptions for *kirpans* to their no-weapons policies. Indeed, in the School Districts of Fremont, Yuba City, Live Oak, and Selma, Sikhs are allowed by virtue of an explicit policy and administrative directive to carry *kirpans* to school, subject to certain conditions.[62]

The cultural politics of *kirpan* remains, despite the judicial activity and legislative record, somewhat elusive. No uniform administrative or legislative policy on *kirpans* in schools exists, and despite the decision by the Court of Appeals, some School Districts will undoubtedly be encouraged by the Governor's veto to persist with policies that would prevent *kirpan*-carrying Sikh children from attending schools. After Wilson's veto, some Sikhs immediately announced that they would continue to pursue their cause, and Ram Singh, one of the leaders of the Sikh community in Fremont, criticized the Governor for obscuring the fact that it is a 'religious freedom issue clear and simple. Wilson is trying to put a spin on it, making it a safety and crime issue so he can use it in his campaign.'[63] Similarly, the author of the bill, Senator Bill Lockyer, has been quite strident in his criticism of the Governor's veto, describing it as another instance of Wilson 'pandering to anti-ethnic groups. Wilson caved into the religious right wing, but when it comes to protecting the religious principles of others, he seems to be completely disinterested.'[64] The supposition that Wilson was merely appeasing the white population shortly before the November 1994 elections is, if anything, kind to him, as there remains the assumption that Wilson is sufficiently pluralistic that he would have, at any other time, assented to the legislation. Lockyer's criticism thus goes further: certain freedoms that are routinely claimed on behalf of Christians are seldom extended to minorities who are practitioners of other religions.

What neither Lockyer's support of the bill, nor ACLU's defense of the right of Sikh children to wear *kirpans* to schools, provides a hint of, is the division of opinion within the Sikh community itself, not to mention other members of the Indian communities in Northern California. One Sikh in Hayward stated quite candidly that entrusting a *kirpan* to a Sikh child is 'like giving a baby a razor blade', and another Sikh opined: 'Someone gets mad and lashes out, and Sikhs get mad really fast.'[65] One other Sikh in the same area thought it was 'not a good idea to carry that [kirpans] in schools. Maybe something may happen with the boys'; and yet another Sikh did not think that if the children failed to carry their kirpans to school, God would be angry with them: 'I still love my religion. But we have to obey the rules and regulations of the country we are living in. The safety—and security—comes first, and everything else comes afterward.'[66]

These remarks scarcely reveal, however, the intense anxieties that have been generated over the entire question of Sikh identity and as I have suggested earlier, the debate over the *kirpan* must also be located in relation to Sikh politics in India, and the revival of the symbols of the faith, particularly among the supporters of Sikh separatism and the adherents of the idea of Khalistan. By the early nineteenth century, Khalsa Sikhs had evolved into a distinct community, the members of which were instructed to have no contact not only with Muslims but with various categories of reprobate Sikhs, including those who disputed the lineage of the Sikh Gurus, and 'those who shaved their heads' and 'did not wear a turban'. In the early part of the twentieth century, 'a ferocious onslaught' was launched against all Sikh men who dared to wear the *dhoti*, a garment associated with Hindus, or who had their ears pierced.[67] Similar attempts to construct boundaries, and to keep the Sikh community 'bound' rather than 'fuzzy', appear to characterize the thinking and practice of orthodox Sikhs today. As has now been well-documented, clean-shaven and 'naked-headed' Sikhs have been the victims of organized attacks, not just in India, but in the US and Canada; and, conversely, in the last ten to fifteen years, the wearing of long hair and unkempt beards has become the most visible mark of one's membership in brotherhood of the Khalsa, the Pure. Veena Das's observations once again come to mind: militant Sikh discourse is characterized by 'use of rigorous dualisms to define self and other', and assertions of masculinity have become central in this discourse. The 'emphasis on ties between *men* as the defining ties of community' is notable; and what is iconic of this masculinity is both the brandishing of the sword (*kirpan*) and keeping one's hair (*kesh*) long.[68] As Bhindranwale was to exhort Sikh males, 'If you do not want beards then you should ask the women to become men and you become women. Or else ask nature that it should stop this growth on your faces.'[69]

Didar Singh Bains, whom we encountered earlier as the world's biggest grower of peaches, and who is one of the most prominent supporters of the idea of Khalistan, certainly appears to have heeded Bhindranwale's counsel: he first took to keeping his hair and beard long in the early 1980s.

He is now committed to proselytization: 'People can't be half pregnant. I got baptized and my wife will one day too.'[70] In her study, published in 1988, of one Sikh community in Northern California, Margaret Gibson noted that 'a split had occurred within the . . . community well before this research commenced, ostensibly because of differences regarding the maintenance of the five Ks and other traditional Sikh values and customs.' She notes that more recent Sikh immigrants to the US have been taking over the gurdwaras, 'insisting that traditional ways be observed'.[71] The same phenomenon can be observed in Canada: here the violence within Sikh communities is attributed to

efforts by younger, more orthodox, more recently-arrived Sikhs to intimidate their fellow Sikhs who are more moderate, more relaxed and resettled in their adopted country. The main thrust has been to capture the existing gurdwaras and through them, order the recovering of the 'naked heads', impose new discipline, control the temple funds—and then proceed toward uniting what traditionally has been a cavalierly disunited overseas Sikh expression.[72]

Thus, among the older members of the Ross Street Gurdwara in Vancouver, a number of men were physically assaulted for being clean-shaven and 'naked-headed'.[73] Since *kirpans* are generally worn under the clothes, an oracular demonstration of militancy among Sikh adults through the brandishing of *kirpans* has not, in California, been an issue, but the whole phenomenon of the revival of the five symbols of the faith has undoubtedly played its part in generating the controversy over *kirpans* in school.

In the discourse on *kirpans* being undertaken by Keshdhari Sikhs in the United States, one claim is directed to members of the Sikh community, particularly to those Sikhs who are construed, by virtue of their failure to keep their hair long or to carry a *kirpan*, as having abandoned the faith. It is not unusual, though hardly reassuring, that Sikhism appears in the diaspora in an ossified and orthodox form, and though the idea of Khalistan has suffered an appreciable decline among Sikhs in India, in the United States the idea of Khalistan continues to have an extraordinary longevity.[74] The 'purer' form of the faith is more easily observed in the diaspora than it is in the 'homeland', where the lived practices of the faith often accommodate themselves to the presence of other faiths sharing family resemblances. This is easily observable in the case of Hinduism as well, and the practices of Hindu associations in the United States suggests that a 'Hindu' is not only more easily defined abroad than at home, but that the parameters of what is allowed to pass for 'Hinduism' are also more narrowly defined. Thus, in a Hindu temple in northern California, access to the deity was restricted by the priest to 'vegetarians', and some latitude allowed to those attired in 'Hindu clothing'. Not much later, the Federation of Hindu Associations calmly conferred its first 'Hindu of the Year' award upon Bal Thackeray, the leader of the Shiv Sena in Mumbai who has been rightfully charged with inciting hatred against the Muslims, and organizing a pogrom, such as the 'riots' of December 1992 and January 1993, against them.[75] This phenomenon cannot be considered with equanimity.

However, the discourse on *kirpans* in the United States contains within it a second claim: one that is directed at members of the dominant white community. The politics of this claim must not be confused with the politics of the disputes within the Sikh faith. Whatever the politics of identity within the Sikh community, the presence of *kirpan*-carrying Sikh children in California's schools has clearly raised other anxieties about identity and cultural politcs. To some observers it is inexplicable that so much heat should have been generated over the subject of *kirpans*, which apparently have so far never been used to inflict violence upon children, when schools have been afflicted with scores of other problems that seem insurmountable. Speaking to a reporter, one leader of the Sikh community in Fremont stated: 'There are a lot of other problems in schools. Why aren't they focusing on them?'[76] The concern over *kirpans* appears to be most prevalent among those, such as conservative legislators and members of the National Rifle Association, who are otherwise keen supporters of the supposed constitutional provision allowing ownership of guns among private citizens, and who have resolutely opposed legislation that would place some restrictions upon the sale and purchase of guns in a country where murder takes the place of civil war and street crime takes the place of terrorism. It is noteworthy that very recently the Supreme Court, in its decision in the Lopez case, gave it as its considered opinion that Congress was not within its jurisdiction in instituting federal legislation banning the possession of guns near schools.[77] If this is the sentiment of the highest court of the land, one might well wonder why the carrying of *kirpans* to school by Sikh children has aroused such controversy and fear.

Significantly, too, the display of religious commitment by the Sikhs, in an age when there are countless other flirtations to amuse the youth, appears to have been one of the principal considerations for support rendered to Sikhs. Describing the *kirpan* as a 'symbol of peace', a 'symbol of forbearance', one lawmaker added: 'I would pray to God my grand-children should go to school with Sikh boys and girls who have the religious commitment the *kirpan* symbolizes.'[78] Similarly, while admonishing the Livingston School authorities for persisting with their ban on *kirpans*, one local newspaper entreated them to 'recognize the fact that these are students of high moral commitment, something to be valued at a time when the enduring values are so lightly held by so many.'[79]

The perception that Sikh children embody, in an age of frivolity and amidst the demise of religion, the virtues of faith and discipline may be overly generous to the Sikh community, and it is even possible to argue that Sikh children who are carrying *kirpans* to school are the victims of a dispute that has arisen within the faith over the meaning of Sikhism and the nature of Sikh identity. Not unusually, children here might be bearing the burden of conflicts and anxieties that adults are unable to resolve. There is also the more pressing consideration whether such a perception, such as that expressed by Christians who envy the Sikhs their resolute religious convictions, can serve as the foundation for a cultural pluralism. It is a telling fact that on three occasions when the Livingston School Board met to discuss the issue before it reached the Courts, not a single non-Sikh family stepped forward in defence of the Cheema family.[80] The successful intervention by the ACLU on behalf of the Cheema family, and the protection accorded to the free exercise of religion by the Constitution and, as it appeared then, the Religious Freedom Restoration Act (RFRA), have aided yet again in obfuscating the limits to liberalism. It is quite clear that the decision of the Court of Appeals, which in any case allowed only an injunction to be issued to prevent the Livingston School District from excluding the Cheema family before the matter came to trial, could just as easily have gone the other way; and the more recent decision of the Supreme Court in 1997 to strike down RFRA as unconstitutional suggests the precariousness of legal victories won at the level of the lower courts. RFRA, in any case, merely restored the tighter criteria for state intervention that should never have been abjured in the first place. The activism of the ACLU and other like organizations serves to retain those liberties for minorities that are constantly being eroded by virtue of judicial conservatism and, more often, the fundamentally conservative ethos of an American pluralism that knows only how to incorporate diversity. When diversity makes demands, and speaks in the language of difference, as have the Sikhs whose children carry *kirpans* to school, the fabric of American multiculturalism is easily shattered. It is no difficult matter to be accommodating of diversity when such 'accommodation' ensures a supply of cheap labour, provides an assurance that the myth of America as the beacon of freedom and the door of opportunity will persist, and in innumerable other ways continues to do the work of maintaining American hegemony. Where assimilation is the prevailing model, claims of diversity are more easily accommodated and diversity even becomes a matter of pride, an instance of the capacity of the nation-state and the people of America to tolerate others. This accommodation does not require an acknowledgement of the Other, and a recognition of the presence of a fundamental and irreconcilable difference.

Legal pluralism, though it momentarily triumphed in the Cheema case, ought not to constitute the limits of cultural pluralism: that has been made all the more clear by the erasure of the Religious Freedom Restoration Act from the statute books. The reliance on Courts, or on administrative fiat, or on legislative remedies, must necessarily constitute part of the panoply of mechanisms available in a democracy for attaining justice, but these avenues for the redressal of grievances do not necessarily make for a pluralistic society. The language of rights has entered the discourse of cultural minorities just as surely as it was stitched into the fabric of Western political thought in the Enlightenment. What has thereby been obscured is the possibility that in lieu of claiming rights, minorities might start thinking of insisting that states be subjected to the fulfilment of certain duties. Rights are claimed against the state, and this has the paradoxical effect of endowing states with agency just when they are being cajoled into disempowering themselves or giving credence to a more equitable mode of distributive justice.[81] The discourse of rights, which puts dominant communities in the position of deliberating upon whether they shall be prepared to endow others with rights, does not compel them to consider their duties, and the interrogation of the Self, which is principally what cultural pluralism should aim at, is never achieved.

The law, it must also be clear, can attempt to provide for equitable conditions of justice, but it cannot produce affection, just as it cannot exercise fear. The fear of the *kirpan* may well be the 'primal' fear of symbols that are not cognizable within one culture's system of significations, but which hint at a politics of which one is dimly aware. Indeed a great deal in the politics of the *kirpan* is unreadable except to those who are well-versed in the politics of Sikhism and the Indian nation-state. The fear of *kirpans*, to raise the specter of untranslatibility, is the fear generated in being unable to understand the language being spoken by one's neighbours: it is the fear of being unable to render the unfamiliar familiar through an act of translation. In a curious fashion, the politics of *kirpans*, while raising important questions about the capacity of Americans to make way for cultural accommodation, also beckons to the politics of Sikhism in India and elsewhere in the diaspora. Thus, by constituting itself as a sovereign discourse, the discourse on *kirpans* marks its independence from American discourses of acculturation and the dominant social framework of understanding.

The question of Sikh identity is central to the conflict over *kirpans* and yet, in some respects, marginal from the American standpoint. None the less, the issue of *kirpans* in schools portends a great deal for understanding what might be the future of cultural pluralism in America. All communities will have to learn to live with a certain degree of *discomfort*, though this idea has not so far entered the discourse of cultural pluralism and multiculturalism. If the fear of the *kirpan* is also the fear of otherness, as I would submit, then perhaps we ought also to accept that otherness cannot always be assimilated, and that living with otherness provides a salutary lesson in formulating a moral code of living. We can applaud diversity, but diversity is easily incorporated, as the American paradigm suggests. Diversity still hints at centripetality: the centre must hold; difference points to centrifugality: the centres radiates outward and dissolves.[82] The privilege of having others being attendant upon their world-view is one that Americans have yet to learn to disown. As the issue of *kirpans* in schools has shown, the true conditions for an *ecological survival of plurality* will only emerge when the fabric of the accepted discourse of diversity begins to unravel.

NOTES

I am extremely grateful to Stephen Bomse, of the law firm of Heller Ehrman White and McAuliffe, for sharing the legal material he had with me. I would also like to express my appreciation of the assistance offered by Bill Lockyer, California State Senator, and Cathy A. Catterson, Clerk of the US Court of Appeals for the Ninth Circuit, and their respective office staffs. My research assistant, Mark Mairot, provided invaluable help in contacting local school boards. This paper was completed in early 1995 and first published as 'Sikh *Kirpans* in California Schools: The Social Construction of Symbols, Legal Pluralism, and the Politics of Diversity', in *Amerasia Journal* 22, no. 1 (1996):57-89.

1. Text of Governor Pete Wilson's veto message, 30 September 1994, on Senate Bill No. 89.

2. Among the conventional authorities in the field, one might enumerate the works of W.H. McLeod, *Guru Nanak and the Sikh Religion* (Oxford: Clarendon Press, 1968), *The Evolution of the Sikh Community* (Oxford: Clarendon Press, 1976), *Early Sikh Tradition* (Oxford: Clarendon Press, 1980), and *The Sikhs: History, Religion, and Society* (New York: Columbia University Press, 1989), and Khushwant Singh's two-volume *History of the Sikhs* (Princeton, New Jersey: Princeton University Press, 1963-6). Some Sikh scholars, I will merely note, have taken strong exception to the work of McLeod, which is sometimes construed as being disrespectful of the faith, while Khushwant Singh's unequivocal condemnation of the violence perpetrated by extremist Sikhs has not endeared him to the more radical members of the community. A more recent history, which dwells largely on the political life of Sikhs in the twentieth century, is Rajiv Kapur, *Sikh Separatism: The Politics of Faith* (Delhi: Vikas Publishing House, 1987).

The recent work of Harjot Oberoi, particularly his *The Construction of Religious Boundaries: Culture, Identity, and Diversity in the Sikh Tradition* (Oxford: Oxford University Press; Chicago: University of Chicago Press, 1994), has been very influential, and is the benchmark against which all future studies of Sikhs and Sikhism before the twentieth century will be judged.

3. See Khushwant Singh, *The Sikhs* (London: George Allen & Unwin, 1953), p. 25. The word guru is most accurately rendered as teacher or master, though in colloquial parlance it has many other usages; *pir* is a Muslim holy man. Numerous words are used to describe the Muslim population of South Asia, and the word 'Mussulman' is used most frequently in Hindustani.

4. See Brian Stock, *The Implications of Literacy* (Princeton: Princeton University Press, 1983), cited by Oberoi, *The Construction of Religious Boundaries*, p. 49.

5. An interesting account of the manner in which the five men were chosen is given in Kapur, *Sikh Separatism*, p. 5. Punjab is from the word *panj*, five, and Punjab is the land of five rivers. The numeral five would appear to have a special significance in Sikhism, there also being five *takhats* (literally, 'thrones') or shrines of authority for Sikhs, mainly associated with the life of Guru Gobind Singh. Moreover, during the baptism of the Sikh child, which is presided over by five Sikh men known for their wisdom and devotion, the sanctified water (*amrit*) is placed on the head of the neophyte, and sprinkled in his eyes, five times, and five times he is given this *amrit* to drink. The *amrit* is itself prepared in an iron bowl where water and sugar crystals are stirred by a double-edged sword: all this is to the accompaniment of the recitation of five quatrains from the writings of Guru Gobind Singh. See Surinder Singh Johar, *Handbook on Sikhism* (Delhi: Vivek Publishing Co., 1977), pp. 105-29, and Oberoi, *Construction of Religious Boundaries*, p. 64.

6. This is scarcely to argue that observance of caste has been eliminated among the Sikhs. As noted by W.H. McLeod, *Who is a Sikh? The Problem of Sikh Identity* (Oxford: Clarendon Press, 1989), 'Whereas the doctrine of the Panth expressly condemns caste, a substantial majority of Sikhs observe certain significant features of caste in practice' (p. 110).

7. J.P. Singh Uberoi, 'The Five Symbols of Sikhism', in Fauja Singh et al., *Sikhism* (Patiala, Punjab: Punjabi University, 1969), p. 129. As can be imagined, I have, for the sake of brevity, given only the most crucial details.

8. Ibid., pp. 130-1.

9. Ibid., pp. 132-3.

10. Ibid., p. 123.

11. Cited by McLeod, *Who is a Sikh?*, p. 98.

12. Uberoi, 'The Five Symbols of Sikhism', p. 136.

13. John Malcolm, 'Sketch of the Sikhs', *Asiatic Researches* 11 (1810): 197-292, at p. 220, cited by McLeod, *Who is a Sikh?*, p. 59. Malcolm did not explicitly mention the five symbols, but the 'arms' must be a reference to the *kirpan*, and the 'steel' to the *kara*.

14. R.W. Falcon, *Handbook on the Sikhs for the use of Regimental Officers* (Allahabad: Pioneer Press, 1896), p. 15, cited by Oberoi, *Construction of Religious Boundaries*, p. 362.

15. Johar, *Handbook on Sikhism*, p. 90.

16. Uberoi, 'The Five Symbols of Sikhism', p. 132. Johar states, in his *Handbook on Sikhism*, that the adoption of the *kirpan* was a 'declaration of sovereignty over oneself

which non-acceptance of restriction on wearing of arms implies'. He adds: 'The deeper spiritual meaning of the *Kirpan* is that it is symbolic of the triumph of transcendental knowledge over ignorance and darkness. The sword, in the mind, cuts at the root of ignorance, evil and worldly attachment and destroys them utterly' (pp. 95-6). This is not an unlikely interpretation, except that Johar leaves it unsubstantiated, besides which it has too much of the tone of an advaitist outlook. The teachings attributed to Guru Gobind Singh, founder of the Khalsa, are really more reminiscent of the teachings of Guru Nanak.

17.   Ratan Singh Bhangu, *Prachin Panth Prakas*, ed. Vir Singh (4th edn., Amritsar, 1962), 16:32-6, cited by McLeod, *Who is a Sikh?*, p. 27.

18.   A militant in the Sikh secessionist movement of recent years tells an interesting story of the consequences he had to suffer upon being inadvertently parted from his sword. One hot summer day, while he was sleeping in his underwear, the sword that slung from a swordband on his left arm slipped off without his being stirred from his deep sleep. Soon thereafter some of his comrades arrived at his home, and were guided by his mother to where he lay asleep; they went back to her, and said: 'Look at this boy, he has been baptized and he has taken a vow to keep the five articles of faith and now he has parted himself from his sword.' Thereupon she replied, 'OK, I'll bring a stick. You beat him with this and teach him that he should be loyal to his faith.' For 'this unconscious conduct' the militant was produced before 'five Sikhs, a sort of court in [the Sikh] tradition', and given 'religious punishment'. See Cynthia Keppley Mahmood, *Fighting for Faith and Nation: Dialogues with Sikh Militants* (Philadelphia: University of Pennsylvania Press, 1996), p. 45.

19.   Oberoi, *Construction of Religious Boundaries*, p. 25.

20.   Kapur, *Sikh Separatism*, p. 92. Though turbans were not numbered among the five symbols of the Sikh faith, by the early part of the nineteenth century, and perhaps slightly earlier, they had become an inextricable part of Sikh identity. W.H. McLeod has written that the wearing of turbans, though lacking 'formal sanction . . . during the nineteenth and twentieth centuries has been accorded an increasing importance in the endless quest for self identification'. The turban became part of the '*Khalsa* code of discipline'. See McLeod, *Evolution of the Sikh Community*, p. 53. For a particularly good discussion of the turban, of the British hand in its place in the creation of Sikh identity, and more generally of the conceptualization of clothes and uniforms during the Raj, see Bernard S. Cohn, 'Cloth, Clothes, and Colonialism', in *Cloth and the Human Experience*, eds. Annette B. Weiner and Jane Schneider (Washington, D.C.: Smithsonian Institution Press, 1989): 303-53 at 304-9.

21.   Kapur, *Sikh Separatism*, pp. 92-3. See also Chap. 7, 'Akali Agitation for Sikh Shrines', in Khushwant Singh, *The Sikhs*, pp. 102-17.

22.   Kapur, *Sikh Separatism*, p. 92. The Punjab Government's report is to be found in the Fortnightly Report, 31 May 1920, in file 95 (Deposit), Home (Political) Proceedings Government of India [henceforth, 'Home Political, GOI'], in National Archives of India [henceforth, NAI], New Delhi.

23.   *The Akali Dal and Shiromani Gurdwara Prabandhak Committee, 1921-22* (Simla: Government Printing, Punjab, 1922), pp. 2, 4, 16, copy in NAI: Home Political, GOI, file 459/II/1922.

24.   NAI: Home Political, GOI, file 459/II/1922, p. 38, 'Brief note on trouble in four Indian units during February 1922.'

25.   Kapur, *Sikh Separatism*, pp. 141-3.

26. NAI: Home Political, GOI, file 459/II/1922, letters from S.P. O'Donnell, Secretary, Home Department, GOI, to Chief Secretary, Punjab Government, 16 and 29 March 1922.
27. 'Exemptions of *Kirpan* from Restrictions under the Arms Act', *Panjab Past and Present* 7, no. 1 (April 1993):162-72.
28. Constitution of India, Article 25, 'Explanation I'.
29. This is, however, an exceedingly loose interpretation of the Constitution, and I have stated it in the form that some Sikhs had accepted. Article 25 reads as follows:

(1) Subject to public order, morality and health and to the other provisions of this Part, all persona are equally entitled to freedom of conscience and the right freely to profess, practise and propagate religion.
(2) Nothing in this article shall affect the operation of any existing law or prevent the State from making any law—
   (a) regulating or restricting any economic, financial, political or other secular activity which may be associated with religious practice;
   (b) providing for social welfare and reform or the throwing open of Hindu religious institutions of a public character to all classes and sections of Hindus.
   Explanation I—The wearing and carrying of *Kirpans* shall be deemed to be included in the profession of the Sikh religion.
   Explanation II—In sub-clause (b) of clause (2), the reference to Hindus shall be construed as including a reference to persons professing the Sikh, Jaina or Buddhist religion, and the reference to Hindu religious institutions shall be construed accordingly.

Clearly, Explanation II cannot be read as a general endorsement of the view that Sikhs, Jains, and Buddhists were to be construed as 'Hindus', and indeed legal experts are agreed that the expanded definition is applicable for the purpose of clause 2(b). This intervention was inspired by the attempt to keep Hindu temples open to the 'untouchables' or Harijans (as they were then called): for example, Harijans who had converted to Buddhism, but who still wished to avail themselves of the right to worship at a Hindu temple, would for that purpose be considered Hindus, and thus be entitled to worship at that temple. According to D.V. Chitaley and S. Appu Rao, *The Constitution of India with Exhaustive, Analytical and Critical Commentaries* (2nd edn., Bombay: The All India Reporter, Ltd., 1970), vol. 2, p. 471, 'Explanation II applies only for the purpose of clause (2) (b), and the expanded definition of Hindus in Explanation II cannot be relied upon for other purposes.'
   It is also important to note that, according to legal opinion, Explanation I envisions that a Sikh may legally carry only one *kirpan*, this *kirpan* to be—in concordance with the articles of Sikh faith—of unspecified length and shape. A *kirpan* is to be allowed to Sikhs as an emblem of their faith, and one *kirpan* suffices as such an emblem. Moreover, 'the Explanation only applies to the particular *kirpan* which is actually used as a religious emblem, but not to a stock of *kirpans* out of which one may be used as an emblem'. Additional *kirpans* may be worn on the procurement of a license, as with any other weapon. See Chitaley and Rao, *Constitution of India*, 2:471, and Durga Das Basu, *Commentary on the Constitution of India* (6th edn., Calcutta: S.C. Sarkar & Sons, 1978), vol. D, p. 232.

30. Cited by Kapur, *Sikh Separatism*, pp. 220-1.

31. For a list of the demands, see Government of India, *White Paper on the Punjab Agitation* (New Delhi: Government of India Press, 10 July 1984), pp. 61-5.

32. See Veena Das, 'Time, self, and community: Features of the Sikh militant discourse', *Contributions to Indian Sociology* (New Series) 26, no. 2 (July-Dec. 1992), p. 252.

33. *White Paper on the Punjab Agitation*, pp. 9-10. The *kirpan* could be no longer than 9 inches, and its blade length was not to exceed 6 inches. It was explained that Sikhs would not be allowed to carry *kirpans* on international flights, as Air India was bound by international regulations and conventions about the carrying of weapons.

34. For two quasi-scholarly accounts of the events of 1980-4, see Kuldip Nayar and Khushwant Singh, *Tragedy of the Punjab: Operation Bluestar and After* (New Delhi: Vision Books, 1984), and Mark Tully and Satish Jacob, *Amritsar: Mrs. Gandhi's Last Battle* (London: Jonathan Cape, 1985). See also the cryptic account by Rahul Kuldip Bedi, 'Politics of a Pogrom', in Arun Shourie et al., *The Assassination and After* (New Delhi: Roli Books, 1985), pp. 51-76. For a short but graphic account of the massacre of Sikhs in Delhi following the announcement of Indira Gandhi's assassination, see People's Union for Democratic Rights (PUDR) and People's Union for Civil Liberties (PUCL), *Who are the Guilty? Report of a Joint Inquiry into the Causes and Impact of the Riots in Delhi from 31 October to 10 November* (Delhi, 1984). It cannot be emphasized enough that the characterization of the carnage of 1-4 November as 'Hindu-Sikh riots' is almost wholly inappropriate. The Sikhs were massacred, and there was no retaliation; nor is it the case that this was preeminently an instance of communalism, for as the PUCL/PUDR report established, the killings were orchestrated by political bosses. For more recent events, from 1984 to 1990, see Man Singh Deora, ed., *Aftermath of Operation Bluestar*, 2 vols. (New Delhi: Anmol Publications, 1992).

I have used the word 'pacification' deliberately, for the ease with which brutal suppression came to be embodied as 'pacification' in the English language is rather remarkable. See George Orwell, 'The Politics of the English Language', *A Collection of Essays* (New York: Doubleday Anchor Books, 1957).

35. Kapur, *Sikh Separatism*, p. 226.

36. Das, 'Time, self, and community', pp. 251-2. On Gandhi's femininity, and his attempted feminization of Indian politics, there is nothing more brilliant than Ashis Nandy's work: 'Final Encounter: The Politics of the Assassination of Gandhi', in his *At the Edge of Psychology: Essays in Politics and Culture* (Delhi: Oxford University Press, 1980; paperback edn., 1990), pp. 70-98, and *The Intimate Enemy: Loss and Recovery of Self under Colonialism* (Delhi: Oxford University Press, 1983), esp. pp. 48-54. A more sympathetic picture of Bhindranwale emerges in Pritam Singh, 'Two Facets of Revivalism: A Defence', in Gopal Singh, ed., *Punjab Today* (New Delhi: Intellectual Publishing House, 1987):167-79 at pp. 169-70, and in the accounts tendered by Sikh militants in Mahmood, *Fighting for Faith and Nation*, esp. pp. 50-72.

37. There is a poignancy in the story of the two men, Sukhjinder Singh and Harjinder Singh, who carried out the assassination of General Vaidya, leader of the Indian armed forces that stormed the Golden Temple in Operation Bluestar and thereby desecrated the venerable shrine. In order to gain membership into Vaidya's golf club, they shaved their beards and cut their hair; and if this should appear to be inexplicable, considering the orthodox fidelity to the Khalsa symbols, it is worthwhile considering

the comment of one Sikh militant that if Sikh men are unable to offer their hair in the Guru's service, how could they conceivably offer their heads? See Mahmood, *Fighting for Faith and Nation*, p. 155.

38. Govt. of India, *White Paper on the Punjab Agitation*, p. 38. For activities of Chauhan, Dal Khalsa, and others, see ibid., pp. 35-40.

39. Bruce La Brack, *The Sikhs of Northern California 1904-1975* (New York: AMS Press, 1988), p. 452.

40. Bruce La Brack, 'California's "Punjabi Century": Changing Punjabi/Sikh Identities', in Pritam Singh and Shinder S. Thandi, eds., *Globalisation and the Region: Explorations in Punjabi Identity* (Coventry: Association for Punjab Studies [UK], 1996), p. 373.

41. La Brack, *The Sikhs of Northern California*, pp. 239, 243-4.

42. Ibid., p. 244.

43. For a brief but lively account of the racism directed against Indians in the US in the first few decades of the twentieth century, see Ronald Takaki, *Strangers from a Different Shore* (Boston: Little Brown and Co., 1989), and a short monograph by Roger Daniels, *History of Indian Immigration to the United States: An Interpretive Essay* (New York: The Asia Society, 1986).

44. California Penal Code, Sec. 626.10 (a).

45. This narrative rests largely upon 'The Brief of Appellants' filed in the Court of Appeals for the Ninth Circuit in the case, No. 94-16097, of *Rajinder Singh Cheema et al., Plaintiffs/Appellants*, v. *Harold V. Thompson et al., Defendants/Appellees*, pp. 1-13. This will hereafter be cited in the body of the paper as 'BOA'. Newspapers were also consulted, particularly the *San Jose Mercury News*, *Oakland Tribune*, and the *San Francisco Chronicle*.

46. I am told that there have been incidents of violence in schools in which the *kirpan* was used, but I have seen no documentary evidence in substantiation of this claim; in the event, such evidence, were it forthcoming, makes no difference to the tenor of my own arguments.

47. As 'The Brief of Appellants' notes, some Sikhs consider the stitching of the handle of the *kirpan* to the cloth strap in which it is carried to be unacceptable, but this was not an issue that the Court had to face, as the Cheemas had agreed to this limitation as a condition for wearing a *kirpan* at school (p. 7, n. 3; see also p. 12, n.7).

48. Religious Freedom Restoration Act of 1993, 42 USC 2000bb. Public Law 103-141 [H.R. 1308], 16 November 1993. Further references to sections of this act will be found in the body of this paper.

49. This case is summarized in Douglas Laycock, 'Free Exercise and the Religous Freedom Restoration Act', *Fordham Law Review* 62, no. 4 (February 1994), pp. 886-8.

50. Laycock, 'Free Exercise and the Religious Freedom Restoration Act', p. 885.

51. Ibid.

52. *Church of the Lukumi Babulu Aye, Inc.* v. *City of Hialeah*, 113 S. Ct. 2217 (1993).

53. See Laycock, 'Free Exercise and the Religious Freedom Restoration Act', pp. 889-92, and Brief of Appellants, p. 15.

54. *Wisconsin* v. *Yoder*, 406 U.S. 205 (1972).

55. *Ray* v. *School Dist. of DeSoto County*, 666 F. Supp. 1524 (M.D. Fla. 1987).

56. Judgement of the Court in *Rajinder Singh Cheema et al.*, v. *Harold H. Thompson et al.*, No. 94-16097, United States Court of Appeals for the Ninth Circuit.

57. Judgement of the Court in *Rajinder Singh Cheema et al.*, v. *Harold H. Thompson*

et al., No. Civ. F-94-5360 GEB, U.S. District Court for the Eastern District of California.

58.   These conditions had previously been agreed to by the Cheemas, though not by the school. The Cheemas agreed that the *kirpan* would be about 6.5-7 inches in length, inclusive of the blade, of a dull type, which was to be 3-3.5 inches; the *kirpan* was to be sewn tightly to its sheath, and was to be worn under the clothes so as not to be readily visible. The school had not agreed to these adjustments proposed by the family. In addition, the Cheema family agreed that a designated official would have the right to make reasonable inspections, and that the right to wear a *kirpan* would be suspended if any of the above conditions were violated; and, finally, it was agreed that the school would take 'reasonable steps to prevent any harassment, intimidation or provocation of the Cheema children by any employee or student in the District. . . .' See ibid.

59.   California Senate Bill 89, 1993-94 Reg. Sess. 626.10 (g) (1993).

60.   Yasmin Anwar, 'Assembly takes up religious knife debate', *Oakland Tribune* (24 August 1994), pp. A9-10; Greg Lucas, 'Bill Allows Sikh Daggers on Campus', *San Francisco Chronicle* (25 August 1994); and 'Senate OKs bill allowing Sikh ceremonial daggers', *San Jose Mercury News* (31 August 1994). In an earlier vote in the Assembly, the bill was defeated 34-14, but as only 48 of the 80 lawmakers had shown up, the vote was rescheduled. As an editorial in the *Oakland Tribune* (24 August 1994) stated, 'the usual small parade of know-nothings, with troglodyte right-wing Republican Ross Johnson of Fullerton out front, led the charge against the bill'. Johnson, charged the newspaper, 'raised the specter of knife fights on school grounds', while Republican Assembly woman Paula Boland claimed that anyone could wear a *kirpan* and claim immunity from sanctions on religious grounds, though the bill specifically rules out that eventuality ('Assembly tramples religious freedom', p. A12).

61.   Text of Governor Pete Wilson's veto message, 30 September 1994, on Senate Bill No. 89. See also Greg Lucas, 'Wilson Veto for Knives at School', *San Francisco Chronicle* (1 October 1994), p. A19.

62.   Personal written communication from Lee Brittenham, Superintendent of Schools, Yuba City Unified School District, 24 January 1995, and from William Walker, Director of Pupil Services, Fremont Unified School District, 8 February 1995.

63.   Suzanne Tay-Kelley, 'Wilson veto of *kirpan* bill has mixed Sikh reaction', *Oakland Tribune* (2 October 1994).

64.   Ibid.

65.   Yasmin Anwar, 'Sikhs on pins and needles over daggers', *Oakland Tribune* (26 April 1994), p. A1, A6.

66.   Tay-Kelley, 'Wilson veto of *kirpan* bill has mixed Sikh reaction'.

67.   See Oberoi, *Construction of Religious Boundaries*, pp. 68-9, 345.

68.   Das, 'Time, self, and community', p. 257.

69.   Quoted in ibid., p. 252.

70.   See Warren Una, *Sikhs Abroad: Attitudes and Acivities of Sikhs Settled in the USA & Canada* (Calcutta: Statesman, 1985), pp. 19-20.

71.   Margaret A. Gibson, *Accommodation without Assimilation: Sikh Immigrants in an American High School* (Ithaca and London: Cornell University Press, 1988), p. 49. She appears to think that the real struggle is over the gurdwaras (pp. 49-50), and thus

the 'ostensible' fight over the symbols, but it is rather curious that she should see the two issues as somehow separate.

72. Una, *Sikhs Abroad*, pp. 33-4.

73. Ibid., pp. 8, 10, 26, and photographs between pages 18 and 19.

74. See Batuk Vora, 'Guns Fall Silent in Punjab, But Khalistan Lingers on in US', *India-West* (10 June 1994), pp. 53, 60.

75. Viji Sundaram, 'Diet, Dress Code Enrage Hindu Worshippers', *India-West* (31 March 1995), Sec. A, pp. 1, 12, 16; for the news item on the 'Hindu of the Year' Award, see *India-West*, issue of 9 June 1995.

76. Jennifer Bjorhus, 'School's Knife Ban Angers Sikhs', *San Francisco Chronicle* (1 August 1994), pp. A1, A12, at A12.

77. 'Excerpts of Justices' Opinions on Ban on Weapons Near Schools', *New York Times* (27 April 1995), Sec. A, p. 16.

78. Greg Lucas, 'Bill Allows Sikh Daggers on Campus', *San Francisco Chronicle* (25 August 1994).

79. 'Abandon the issue: No point in Livingston pursuing the school knife ban', editorial in *The Modesto Bee* (8 September 1994), p. A8.

80. Bjorhus, 'School's Knife Ban Angers Sikhs', p. A12.

81. For a more extended consideration of this issue, see Vinay Lal, 'The Imperialism of Human Rights', *Focus on Law Studies* 8, no. 1 (Fall 1992): 5ff.

82. Arjun Appadurai, in 'Patriotism and Its Futures', *Public Culture*, no. 5 (1993):411-29, suggests quite brilliantly why the idea of immigration, which represents centipetal forces, now appears less attractive than the idea of diasporas, which are generated by centrifugal forces.

These are not Symbols

The earth on that day was parched and brown, the roads were unusually deserted of the traffic and even the construction workers, otherwise so busy and undaunted by the heat were looking for a shade to rest in. It was a very hot and humid day. In the well manicured lawns of an elitist college in the Delhi University, many students were stretched out on the grass or sitting on the worn out wooden benches under a cluster of Banyan trees. They were taking cold drinks and gasping for fresh air. The clouds were grey, there was not even a whisper among the tired trees, and the earth itself seemed to have failed in its rotation. You could touch the heat, feel it, smell it and it seemed to trap you.

To fight the heat, and the sweat, everyone in the college lawns was busy talking, except for Jaskirat Singh who was sitting all alone, contemplating under the thatched roof of the motorbike shed. He was tall, well built, sharp featured and looked very distinctive with his bright red turban, bearded chin and a jet black cavalier moustache. One could hardly imagine, what his imported jeans must have looked like when he first wore them two years back because now they were held together by a series of patches of various dimensions ranging from a traingle to a hexagon.

Jaskirat was from a fairly affluent family of Punjab and had been residing in a hostel for the last eleven years, going home only for the summer and winter vacations. From his school days he had been very interested in his studies and was always among the first three, in his class. A voracious reader, an excellent sportsman, the most sought after orator in his college, a member of the college students' union, he always strived for perfection in whatever he tried. But now in his final year of M.A. though still quite young, he felt he had lost the spark of life. He carried on his work almost mechanically, going through the monotonous routine with boredom, there was no longer any zest in what he did and the drive which he had once felt, was completely gone. He was confused, lonely and almost angry with himself.

His friends did not consider him to be 'hep' enough (a slang word often used by students for one who is completely Westernised in his manners, values of life and is well experienced in psychedelic experiences; in short a product of the Hi-Fi culture), and this was certainly a drawback, as it was the degree of hepness which an individual could imbibe, however artificial the attempt or the result might be, which provided the key to the all-night parties and was a measure of the upward social mobility among the student community. Jaskirat's flowing beard, his untrimmed moustache and his refusal to join his friends in drinking bouts and smoking joints of marijuana earned him the nickname of 'Sant Maharaj ji'! 'Dont you smoke?' Was a query which he was often faced with and before he could reply he was told, 'Come on, you must be smoking in your room, all Sikhs do. Go ahead, we are not going to write to your old man.' When Jaskirat, told his friends that he did not smoke, they were not pleased with him and were not ready to take his word. They called him a 'hypocrite' behind his back. But his ostracization in the campus did not end here; the pressures were increasing every day. Amrita Kaur, popularly known 'Miss I.Q.', a classmate of Jaskirat and a good friend of his, was unwilling to accept his invitation for a party, because he insisted on carrying a *kirpan* with him to the party, which for her was a sign of cultural shallowness and crudeness of the mind. Such behaviour for her was certainly an obstacle in his endeavour to be one with the 'In-Crowd'. She was in no mood for a compromise this time and was determined to put him in a tight spot. In her intellectual anger she tersely told him, 'You claim to be progressive in your views, you talk of the natural law of development to higher forms of existence, but still you carry a sword like a feudal hero, who is not ready to give up his obsolete armour. If it is for self-defence and honour, which you are so fond of claiming, in that case a gun would be anytime more efficient to do the job. Live in the present, do not be a priest of the past'. A note slipped by her in Jaskirat's room in the hostel offered him a job of a 'Moral Science teacher in a Convent School.

The more Jaskirat tried to untangle his problem, the more he was convinced of the futility of his attempts. Once he had been proud in his capacity of employing logic and reason to unravel the mysteries of life, but now even this powerful and convincing pair, betrayed him. Unable to carry on with the ever increasing pressure of his tight rope walking, he decided to write to his father who had always been keen to see his son happy, at peace with himself and above all, a *Guru ka Sikh*. Jaskirat was fortunate to have as his father a famous poet, who had been honoured with several coveted awards both within and outside India. During the past thirty years, he had steadily become known through his many books as one of the most stimulating and unconventional poets of our time. He had been a lecturer of Cambridge Harvard's Michigan and had spoken before various international associations and institutions.

The correspondence between the father and the son had always been a great source of inspiration, courage and confidence for Jaskirat and he always used to read aloud, to his friends the letters from his father. When his books, friends and teachers failed him, he invariably turned to his father. This had been a regular feature with him since he was six and had learnt to write English. When he was seven year old, he had wanted to know how he could run faster; at twelve he wanted to know, how he could develop a sharper memory and now at twenty when he wanted to know why he should be duty bound to keep long hair and carry a sword? It was this dilemma which seemed to be eating him up and leaving him in a paralysed state. The cure he knew, if there was, only available with his father, to whom he must write about his ailment. In writing to his father he felt like a rebel, an insult to his family, a traitor to his community. But the jigsaw puzzle had to be solved whose pieces he himself was in no position to put together.

St. Stephen's College
Rudra South
Delhi, May 1977

My dear Dad,

Sat Sri Akal. It is with extreme pain, conflict and misery that I am writing to you. I feel utterly empty, almost naked, my heart weary, dull and isolated. This could have been another one of those nice and happy letters, which we both have been writing to each other all these years. But all those nice things seem to be happening no more. Happiness, which completely ravished my heart once, has gone and now I have only the empty memory of it. I seem to have lost the intimate contact with life. I must apologize, for suddenly bursting forth like this and for not having written about my problems all these months. But till about a week back I was lonely when the books which I so patiently read, all those self proclaimed gurus I went to see and hear, and my own experience and reasoning failed me, that I resolved to write to you Dad, my inability to accept the five Ks, which all my life till now, seemed to be so crucial for me in my effort to be a God-fearing man, a religious man, a dutiful son and above all *Guru ka Sikh.*

I have no doubt and am not questioning about the efficacy of these symbols three centuries ago when they were essential in times of war to maintain the identity of Sikhs and give them a common denominator of unity and togetherness. It was a good strategy for fighting against an enemy bent on destroying the very seeds of Sikhism. But for the present these symbols have no justification, no meaning nor any convincing explanation. Not only has it become difficult for me to explain the relevance of a *kirpan* or a *kara*, but also for those who sermonize in the gurdwaras or those who so zealously write in the religious magazines. Sardar Ganpartap Singh wrote a five page article on the utility of the five Ks, but when I met him at club last month, he was definitely not carrying a *kirpan*. He is no exception in these double standards.

It is not me alone who has felt this lacuna, but most Sikh boys in my college (Rajbir, Suchet, Mandeep) are also unable to accept these symbols and their validity for everday life. They can establish no coherent connection between a *kirpan* and the human effort for communion with God. In no way can I convince them that these symbols make me more of a Sikh than them. They are as much recognized as Sikhs as I am. In fact more so because they are seen to be in tune with the modern times whereas I am looked upon as a romantic idiot who sees in the idealistic past and in a set of five symbols a stepping stone for him liberation in the future. The belief in God, the need for a deeper consciousness, the harm in smoking, the ill-effects of drinking, the daily reading of the *Japji*—all these I have no objections to and fully agree with, but the five symbols do not fit into any logical framework for a happy classical Hinduism. Manu, the Hindu law giver, lays down:

'Even should a man be in wrath let him never seize another by the hair. When a brahmin commits an offence for which members of other castes are liable to death, let his hair be shaven off as sufficient explanation.' The keeping of the hair is regarded as an indicator of living in accordance with the way of nature; the shaving of the hair it is maintained is an interference with the natural law of the growth of hair. A latest book published on Sikhism by a premier university of Punjab emphasizes that the keeping of the hair was a part of the Sikh ritual which was life affirming, an indicator of the Sikhs' commitment to a social and worldly life in contrast with the Hindu sanyasis and jogis who cut their hair because they professed to the creed: 'I am no one's and no one is mine'. The Sikhs in contrast were to be a part of the world and to affirm this worldly existence they were instructed to keep long hair while the sanyasis shaved their head, beard and moustache, before entering the new ascetic phase of their life. The cutting of the hair is thus seen as a social death. The Sikh community on the other hand was an affirmation of the normal social world. 'As the battle ground of freedom.' The meaning of being unshorn, therefore, signifies according to the book: 'the permanent renunciation of renunciation'.

Various articles emphasize on the hair being a living organ of the body and to cut them is seen as depriving the body of an essential source of vitality. The hair is seen as a contact point with the sun, the basic source of universal energy. One author cites the authority of C.G. Jung and claims that the Guru Sahib was a great psycho-analyst and he asked the Sikhs to keep hair so as to confirm the instinct of masculinity, from which man at time deviates. To convice the youth, some influential speakers stress on the scientific validity of hair, but without any empirical data to substantiate their statements. Others see the hair as a symbol of virility, honour, power, aggression and so on.

THE *KANGHA* (COMB)

The *kangha* is explained in utilitarian terms, as a means to keep the hair neat and clean. It is also seen as a symbol of the discipline of mind. In a flight of imagination, one author writes in a magazine published from Calcutta, that by wearing the comb, the Sikh should be reminded to keep his mind under control, his thoughts should not be allowed to wander aimlessly, his mind should be kept orderly, methodological and well disciplined. The *kangha* is seen as a fetter to excessive anger or excessive attachment. (It is not explained how?) Most writers dismiss its significance in one line and see it as a twin of the long hair.

THE *KACHHA* (UNDERPANT)

The case of *kachha* is even more interesting. An eminent writer, writes in a book sponsored by the Government of India, that the *kachha* is for a smart wear as against the loose unstitched *dhoti* worn earlier. Strangely, reading the mind of Guru Sahib, it is claimed that the loose *dhoti* represented to the Guruji a loose mentality. By providing the Sikhs with the shorts it was intended to symbolize the spiritual and mental breakway from traditional dress and thought. The mind was to be freed from the bonds of superstitions and the people were thus to be released from immature and effeminiate submissiveness. They were destined to become mature, solid and active soldiers. Hence, the symbol of the *kachha* was same for the Sikh women they were also intended to develop the same qualities as Sikh men. (I fail to understand why the same qualities were to be developed through the medium of the *kachha*). The *kachha* is also seen as a symbol of control over excessive sexual indulgence.

THE *KIRPAN* (SWORD)

The *kirpan* is made out to be a symbol of royal authority and of feedom from oppression and servility. Its obvious meaning is stated to be that of self defence and the individual freedom and self respect, embodied in the right to wear arms. The sword it is said, cuts at the root of evil and worldly attachment and destroys them utterly. The primary significance is said to be that of self defence, with a word of caution that it is not an instrument of aggrandizement but self protection.

THE *KARA* (IRON BANGLE)

A Sikh journalist in his account of the Sikhs writes that the *kara* was a symbol of humanity as well as a charm worn before going to the war. On the other hand a senior Sikh historian feels that the *kara* denotes the universality of the new religion. In a very appealing reasoning it is also argued that the complete unbroken circle symbolizes the Buddhist 'Wheel of Life'. The spiritual reality of life exists continually, free of both time and space and the *kara* is an appropriate symbol of such eternal existence. The human soul, it is instructed, must become as strong as steel used in the *kara* which has been tempered in the furnace. The other day a Bhai in the gurdwara insisted that the genius of Sri Guru Gobind Singhji was reflected in his providing us with a steel *kara*, which can protect us from lightening. A student speaking on the relevance of the five Ks felt that the *kara* was to protect the arms in the battlefield from the sword cuts. It was an excellent shield for the arm according to him.

The explanations for Ks are a paradise of pick and choose. One may choose the one which an individual fancies the most, very much like a nice trouser in a show window. It is not strange if some think that the choice is still not wide enough to appeal to their senses. So they come out with the choice of discarding these symbols. If I take the view that the *kirpan* is for self-defence, can I discard it, if I have twenty bodygaurds with all the latest equipment for protecting my life? Again if an individual feels that if the *kirpan* is for self-defence, as is so often told to him by the historians, in that case he can hypothetically argue that he should be allowed to do away with it, because he feels that the state has made adequate arrangements for his protection.

Daddy, I am utterly incapable of understanding the value, the justification and the imposition of these symbols. I am deeply hurt but am unable to find any medicine for my wounds. The cures which have been suggested have further aggravated my malady. The numerous explanations given for these symbols seem to be like so many needles pricked into my body. The books, the Bhais, the glossy magazines, the well-meaning speakers, have all failed me and I turn to you not only because you are my father but also because of your deep commitment, understanding and love for the Sikh way of life.

I understand, it is going to be a long, weary and difficult way to a deeper understanding of these symbols, but I am prepared to jump into the arena and take the challenge and I give you my word that in case you can show me the way and the significance of these symbols, I will not hesitate for a moment to go to Sri Anandpur Sahib and be an Amritdhari Sikh. We have established a unit of Guru Gobind Singh Study Circle here in our college and I will put all the explanation before my co-workers.

With lots of love

Your loving son
Jaskirat Singh
Cornell University
New York, USA
15 June 1977

Dearest Jaskirat,

Sat Sri Akal. I must thank you for the deep confidence and the love you have for me. It has always been a joy to read through your letters as they manifest the sensitivity of a seeker of truth. I am very happy that you had the courage and conviction to express so openly the things that seem to have been distressing your heart. I somehow felt all this brewing up in you, for the last two years, but had never allowed myself to face it directly, till you wrote the present letter. It is a pleasure to hear it all so plainly stated, and I hope, I shall understand and calm your mental anguish.

When you leave the university and face the world it seems to me that what is crucial in life is not to succumb, not to bow your head to various pressures, but to know and feel them as they are, in a gentle spirit, with a great inward strength, so that these pressures will not create conflict in your life. You may question what is given to you or what many of your age assert is being forced on you—but this also means that you must question yourself. You must not merely question, what you call the significance, the need, the value of your own life. It is only with such an integrated total approach that you will understand not only the *kirpan*, the *kara*, the *kangha* the *kesh*, and the *kachha*, but also appreciate the agonies, the joys, the pain, the pleasure, the vanities and hope of living.

The whole world, all your friends, your relations, everyone is struggling for significant and useful things. But what might be significant for you might not be so for your friends.

If you go to a man who has ill-health, he will undoubtedly say, what is significant is good health. If you go to a man who has not had enough wealth all his life, he will say what is significant in life is money. If you go to a mother she will say the significant thing is to have a son. This is the reason to find an intricate web of explanations, for the significance of five Ks. Every one views it from his own angle of significance.

The first step in your questioning of the five Ks should be to be free of this yoke of significance. It is this illusionary search for significance which has made many young ones and their seniors, discard their *kesh* because they see no value in them. It is a pity that we want to reduce Sahib Guru Gobind Singhji, to our own mundane level of thinking and view all his actions in the light of practical animal utility. If he was in search of merely objects of practical utility, he could have made a truce with Aurangzeb, when the latter made the offer. Shivaji did so at one stage, because his search was different, in his life. If the rider of the dark blue steed, wanted the five Ks to be reflections of practical use values, he could very well have added not only more weapons, but instead of a sword, he would have given us a gun, as guns did exist at that time. A gun would have been more efficient and better suited for self-defence and for war too. But he was not inspired out of a hunt for weapons of self-defence or practical value, as we would make it out, reflecting our own thinking backwards in history. The Guru Sahib was not a novice in the ways of the arms, if he only wanted his Sikhs to be armed for war, through these five Ks. He would have rather equipped them that way, like he did Banda Bahadur at Nanded, when he gave him five arrows and a bow. The sword, anyway, in the battlefield would have been useless without a shield.

The *kangha*, the *kesh*, the *kara*, the *kirpan* and the *kachha* were all delicate gifts of love and beauty to the Khalsa from his Master who desired nothing for himself, but everything for the Khalsa. These gifts were from a Guru who grabbed not the gifts of his disciples but instead totally surrendered everything for the cause and love of the Khalsa.

A way of total love which was to be unique for the Khalsa: '*Jau tau prem khelan ka chao sir dhar tali gali meri ao'* (Guru Nanak Devji), 'If thou art zealous of playing the game of love, then enter upon my path with thy head on thy palm.' It was out of such love that these gifts were presented to the Khalsa and not out of any attempt to carve out soldiers. When there is total love there is action, there is sacrifice. Is it not so? The love of Guru for the Khalsa was not the result of mental vibrations, and there was in his life no gap between love and action, as there is between our thinking and action. It is only we who want to be one sided in our love and make claims of loving the Guru in our ideals, in our heart and consequently we reason out that we do not have to express our love for him in action, in the *kesh*. But can there be love of Kalgidhar Guru Gobind Singhji for the Khalsa become apparent in the book titled *Sarbloh*, where, he becomes one with the Khalsa and portrays the Khalsa as his highest love:

> Khalsa is the breath of my body,
> Khalsa is the very soul of my life,
> Khalsa is my real pride and glory,
> Khalsa is my own personal self,
> Khalsa is my life's sustainer,
> Khalsa is my body and breath,
> Khalsa is my creed and karma,
> Khalsa is my conscience keeper.
> Khalsa is my perfect *Satguru*,
> Khalsa is my brave friend,
> Khalsa gives me intellect and wisdom,
> Khalsa is my object of meditation.

The mind that loves the Sikh way of life is a religious mind because it is the movement of living, of action, of truth, of God, and it is only such a mind that can know what is the beauty of gifts the Guru gave to us. The five ornaments that we wear are the gifts from the Guru, whose two younger sons, seven and nine years old, faced martyrdom in Sirhind in a manner which is unequalled in the long annals of human history. These two innocent children were walled alive because they refused to bow before the sword of hatred. The Guru's mother merged into the Supreme Being at Sirhind during persecution. The two elder sons of the Guru countered martyrdom fighting in action for us. Guru Sahib himself had been attacked with dagger by two cowardly Pathans at Nanded in Deccan, causing serious injury.

Could such a benevolent being whose whole family was destroyed for the total love of the Khalsa, be looking for practical utilities of an animal existence? He was not the person to endow us with gifts of mere practical value, but gifts of love, which knew no questioning, no bartering, no deals and no betraying. His was a total sacrifice and a total love in both thought and action, for the happiness of the Khalsa and these gifts had their pangs of birth in a sea of human blood. It was not out of any practical benefit that the evil genius of the Mughal government announced rewards for the hair of Sikhs. It was because they knew that without these gifts, without these emblems of the Guru's love, the Khalsa would disintegrate.

All the children of the Khalsa are to always wear a sword, which in no way is, their own private possession or property. The *kirpan* is a gift from Guru Gobind Singhji to the Khalsa. It is not to be judged and measured as a weapon of war or peace, it is a gift activated by the love of the Guru. Even a whole army of bodyguards of the best police state in the world cannot make it redundant. The *kirpan* shall always remain attached to me, the bodyguards cannot make it obsolescent. The sword is the love wherein the Guru resides. A Guru who in his love saw no difference between human beings and fused all of us in one creed of devotion, service and sacrifice, in an age when common men were hanged for even drawing water from the same well as that of the higher castes. The lower castes were beaten to death if they as much touched the kitchen utensils of a Brahman.

A *Kalal*, a wine distiller, once came for the Guru's *darshan* and stood at a distance, for the caste of the *Kalal* was considered low in the social hierachy.

When Guru Gobind Singhji, saw him, he said, 'Come in and sit with all of us in the tent.' The man quivered, hesitated and said, 'How can I, the lowliest of the low, sit in the assembly of the gods? Guruji, I am a *Kalal* whose mere sight pollutes.' On hearing this, Guru Sahib instructed his musicians and bards to welcome the man with music and songs, and coming down from his couch to bless him, he said, 'You are not a *Kalal*, but a "*Guru ka Lal*", a "Ruby of the Guru".' Who has such love for us? The sword which we have is an ornament for all of us, the rich and the poor, you, me and the whole humanity. To wear a sword which was once a privilege of the few high born, under the dictates of the Mughal aristocracy, with the Guru's blessings became a gift which anyone could carry, without fear of being prosecuted, because now it was in love from the Guru to the Khalsa '*dan dio iniko bhalo avar anko dan na lagat niko.*' (Guru Gobind Singh), 'To bestow gifts on them alone is worthy, to make gifts to others is not kind.'

When his hands stroked our hair, washed them, combed them, knotted them and placed in them the invaluable *kangha*, how can we, his sons and daughters, bear our hair to be cut? The Guru Sahib saturated our hair with *amrit*. He left the imprint of his blessings and joy in our hair. Our hair is like the untouched pearl in the deep oceans not yet disfigured by the fortune hunters. You say it is inconvenient, frustrating, impractical to grow our hair long. But more frustrating is an existence of no inspiration, no effort. Our superficial hollow life is in no way less discouraging. The day to day fragmentary living, the everyday struggle for food, the daily pain, suffering, distress, torments and headaches are in no way less discomforting. But in spite of all this do we cease to exist? No, on the contrary we strive all the more and struggle for pleasure, gratification, comforts, and joy. If we can reconcile ourselves to such an empty living, can we not grow our hair long which is so inspiring, creative, fulfilling and above all a gift from our Guru, a gift whose rejection would be a rejection of our existence, the negation of the very purpose of our life.

In the West, the children love so much the gifts made to them on Christmas by the mythical Santa Claus. They eagerly search their stockings for the gifts placed in them by their parents and after receiving their gifts feel so elated; and we are so ungrateful, that we fight, throw away, kick at the gifts of our loving father, who kept nothing for the future of his house and gifted to us everything he possessed—physical, spiritual and material.

The elegant *kachha* we wear every day is the very same as the one worn by Guruji himself, by his disciples and by his lovers. Clad in it, we are one with him. The exotic wooden comb he tucked in our hair, also combed, danced and swung in his hair. The *kangha*, is the new born baby, playing in the lap of the loving mother, whom we so brutally want to strangle. It was these very presents, for which hundreds and thousands of my brothers laid down their lives. Have you watched the tears in the eyes of the sheep while she is being sheared? And many of us are so happy without our hair. We for sure, have travelled a long way from the animal.

The *kara* has to be received by us as a present from our Guru, which is not comparable to our wealth, our intelligence, our achievements. It comes to us as a manifestation of his love and benefaction. It is strange behaviour indeed that we constantly argue about it. He put on our wrist the *kara*, from that day it was for ever ours; no one could separate it from a Sikh. And we still advance reasons for it. He loved me. He made me his own. He elevated me from the darkness of ignorance to the light of spiritual consciousness. Can I not even make his gifts my own? We, his children, have to wear these gifts, carved out of infinite love. One with these gifts, we blossom; separated from them, we wither. The decay in the Khalsa is apparent.

Each one of us wears the hair and beard of Guru Gobind Singhji, exactly as he wore them. We are created in his majestic image. *'Jab lag khalsa rahe niara, tab lag tej dio mai sara, jab eh gahain bipran ki riti, mai na karo in ki partit'* (Guru Gobind Singh), 'So long as the Khalsa retains identity, I will bestow on them full glory; but the moment they adopt Brahmancial ways, I will not protect them.' Our significance is in him, and not everywhere without him and his gifts. In these gifts we are reminded of his Omniscience, Omnipotence and Omnipresence.

Jaskirat, do not make our presents into dead symbols, they are the gorgeous ornaments of the living. We are the 'Wedded Women', of the God. They are the wedding gifts from our Bridegroom. He gave all of them to use and they are God sent—imperishable, indispensable and indestructible. But the waves of pure love always have their own logic, rationality and fatalism. I love the Guru's irrationality—if you want to call it so, *'sev kari in hi ki bhavat, aur ki sev suhat na jiko'* (Guru Gobind Singh), 'To serve them pleaseth me, service of any other is not dear to me' I don't have the courage to reject such devotion.

Does a would-be-wife question the intrinsic value of the engagement ring, she is gifted by her husband? No, never, even if it is made of copper or a shell. Today, you want to discard these gifts, because gold has more value. Yes, iron was poor in worldly goods. A wealthy merchant, Hargopal, once grudgingly brought for Guru Gobind Singh, two gold bracelets studded with precious jewels, not because he loved the Guru, but because he felt that in doing so, he would please his own father, who was a devotee of the Guru Sahib. One of these expensive bracelets accidently fell into the Yamuna river from the hands of Guruji. At this, Hargopal was very displeased and when his attempt to recover the bracelet proved futile, he asked Guruji to point at the exact place where he had dropped the bracelet, so that he could take it out. To indicate the place in the river where the bracelet had fallen, Guru Gobind Singhji took out the other gold bracelet, from his wrist and throwing in the river he told Hargopal, 'It is there.'

You want to question the utility of the 'iron bangle of the Guru, but not of the gold bangle which is so much in vogue at Sikh engagement ceremonies today. You are ready to discard the Guru's bangle for the yellow metal. But do not forget your first marriage, out of whose womb you stand today, aspiring for these worldly gifts. The body can be made the basis of either animal incontinence or a divine temple. The choice is yours, the consequence are yours. The bliss of love is yours, the solitude of separation is yours. These gifts are not to be stored in the darkness of the cellars; think deep into them, if you want to live in spiritual grandeur.

The head of a Sikh, the *kesh* of a Singh, having been once offered and accepted, became forever of the Guru. It is an unceasing trust with him. It is, therefore, imperative for a Sikh to carry his head high and not to bow it before a mortal barber. It shall only bend and bow before the Guru. Once a new musket was brought as a present, for Guru Gobind Singhji. He said, to test the love of his disciples, that he wanted to try the aim of musket on some one's forehead. He looked around and asked if any of his Singhs would offer himself for the trial. Quick came up scores of unflinching Sikhs, each pushing the other one away, regarding it as a boon to meet death at the Guru's hand. And today we are so uninspired, sleeping beauties, that except for empty words, have no deeds worthy of our name.

Everyday we recite in our prayer, '*Nanak das sada Kurbani.*' 'Nanak thy servant is ever a sacrifice to Thee.' But what is it that we sacrifice everyday? Guru Gobind Singh was the purest sacrifice. We may never reach his height, but some sacrifice we can make. But instead we sacrifice our five Ks. Shocking is our spirit of sacrifice. If the Khalsa today is hollow, it is because we forget the love of a sacrificer, it is because we regard his gifts as mere symbols. '*Balhari Gur apne diohadi sadvar.*' (Guru Nanak), 'I am sacrifice to my Guru hundred times a day.' Are we the worthy inheritors of this heritage? After drawing on his blood, now we want to stab him in the back!

Jaskirat, one kilometre from the Lahore railway station stands a gurdwara sacred to the Sikhs in the loving memory of Bhai Taru Singhji. It bears the name of Shahid Ganj, the Abode of Martyrs. Bhai Sahib was resident of village Poola, where he had a small piece of land. The wheat and the maize that he produced and the humble mud hut he had, he happily shared with all the weary travellers who passed through the village and needed a shelter to sleep for the night. He belonged wholly to the Guru's hymns and early in the morning under the stars, while on the plough, with a white turban and a blue *chola*, a poor toiler of the earth, he recited the *Japji*. The *Japji* has in it the inimitable cosmicness of life in nature. The villagers loved Taru Singh for his fellow feeling, harmlessness and spiritual purity.

But being a Sikh, Taru Singh was not destined to live any longer his life of love, free from the hatred of caste, colour and religion. The authoritarian Mughal government of medieval India was not willing to appreciate the way of life of the Sikhs, which drew no dividing line between man and man, between Hindus and Muslims, between Brahmans and Sardars, '*manas ki jat sab ek hi pahchanbo*' (Guru Gobind Singh), 'All men are the same', was a creed which cut at the very root of Mughal establishment based on human distinctions. To extinguish this smithy of love, the government offered to its subjects numerous monetary awards for the heads of the Sikhs and they were declared outlaws. The greed for gold tempted Bhagat Niranig to lodge a complaint against Bhai Taru Singh with the Subedar (governor) of Lahore, stating that he gave shelter to dacoits, the Sikhs, and the property of Muslim and Hindu subjects of His Gracious Majesty was unsafe. Such a complaint was unnecessary for the very living of a Sikh was a reason enough for the state armed forces to go and imprison Bhai Taru Singh, who was bound in ropes and brought before the Subedar.

When the Subedar saw this youngman of 23, he was overwhelmed and shaken by his presence. He felt himself.transposed to another world. There was a radiance around him which made the Nawab exclaim: '*Khuda*! What a divine *Noor* (glory) on his face. I pray that he should be a Musalman!' Addressing Taru Singh, the Nawab Said, 'O, graceful Sikh, I feel sorry for you and I wish to give you a new lease of life.'

Taru Singh with tears in his eyes, responded: 'Reward me with a new lease of life? Why stain me with such dishonour while my brothers and sisters are being martyred here before me, every day, every hour?'

The Subedar said, 'Your presence is resplendent with a heavenly light. Somehow my heart does not permit me to have you killed, but you must cut and present me your tress-knot.'

Taru Singh replied, 'The Sikh and his hair are one. I will be pleased to give you more than you ask me, my head with my tress-knot. These hair are the eternal gift of love, of immeasurable beauty to the Khalsa by our Guru; they cannot be separated from a Singh's head, without separating his head. The one who just looks at them can never understand them. It is like looking into a mirror, but you are not one with the mirror. The observer is only capable of experiencing, he is never a mirror, the experience, the state itself. These hair are the fountain of joy, the spring of life for us.'

The Subedar still confident of bribing him, then said, 'Taru Singh, you are too young, You have not yet experienced the beauty and joy of life. I will make arrangements for your marriage with a woman of your choice. You will be awarded with high *mansab* (office) in the Mughal army. You will be endowed with a hereditary *jagir*. I promise you all sorts of luxuries but you must part with your way of life and accept the Muslim religion.'

A Guru *ka* Sikh can never be tamed and now his tears mingling with a smile of joy, Taru Singh replied, '"Having been sent by Him they come (into the world) and recalled by Him they go back", said Guru Nanak. "It is the right and privilege of the brave to die," says He, 'for a Sikh, life has beginning and no end—it is both death and life. Neither my life nor my hair are for bargaining in your court which views beauty, life and religion in weights of gold. The value and beauty of our hair cannot be measured in terms of luxuries and *jagirs*. Your thinking is materialistic and is therefore negligible, but an integrated living is always spiritual.'

The Subedar could no long bear this song of truth and he cried out, 'Stop him, for he disturbs the law and order of our province. Kill him at once, but cut his hair before.'

The Mughal soldiers caught hold of Bhai Sahib's head and chin, but the barber found it impossible to bring his hand near his head. With a stroke of his head he would push back his captors and make them whirl on the ground. A cobbler was then sent for, to try his skill with his tools and scrape of Taru Singh's hair, but his attempt too proved abortive. At last the help of a carpenter was asked for the foul deed. With a stroke of his axe, he cut off Bhai Taru Singh's head (AD 1743) but failed to cut his tress-knot.

Thakur Rabindranath Tagore, a great mystic poet of Bengal, has beautifully sung of this episode in *Parathona Atit Dan* ('More than asked for'):

> For a Sikh to cut his tress-knots
> Amounts to discarding his dharma
> The Pathans brought, bound hand and
> foot, the Sikh prisoners,
> Shahid Ganj earth turned red
> with their blood the Nawab addressing Taru Singh,
> said unto him:
>
> 'I wish to spare thy life.'
> Taru Singh retorted: 'Spare my life!
> Why thou dishonour me?'
> Said the Nawab: 'Thou art bravest
> of the brave?
> I don't wish to wreak my anger
> on thee.'
> Taru Singh replied: 'O Nawab thy
> request with my heart I comply
> and liberally grant thee more than
> what thou beg of me:
>
> My head with my tress-knot.'

Jaskirat, if Bhai Taru Singh had looked for practical utility, significance and relevance wouldn't he have exchanged his hair for a *jagir*, for beautiful women and the power he was offered? But all these he regarded as worthless when he weighed them with his way of life. If the hair were mere symbols for him, would he have staked his life for them. The term symbols can never express the depth of these gifts.

You will never find even a most dutiful policeman leaping to death, to uphold a short circuited, burning, traffic light signal, because it is a sheer symbol for the cars and lorries on the road, it is an external factor to his life. But our five Ks are much deeper and profound than symbols and this is the reason we find not only Bhai Taru Singh, but a whole galaxy of martyrs in our history—Bhai Mati Das and Dyal Chand, Bhai Mani Singh, Bhai Bota Singh, Sardar Mehtab Singh, Sukha Singh and Subeg Singh—all playing with their lives, which appears to us so irrational and fatalistic.

Son, you merely read about the five symbols in isolation; now meditate on them as links with lives of your ancestors, for it is only then that their meaning will be apparent to you. In themselves the five Ks might appear to be mere symbols, show windows, but it is only when they are knit with our lives, woven in our existence, painted with our daily sorrow and joys that their value, justification and significance emerges. They are inseparable from our life and if you perceive them as separate, it is not surprising that they appear to be frivolous, unjustified and a burden of the past. If you are wounded and in agony, it is because you want to separate, from yourself, what is vital for existence.

Unfortunately, you visualized only a part in segregation from the whole. You are looking out of a small window set in the wall, from which the outside may appear to be attractive and convincing sometimes, but does not allow you to view the beauty of life. Without linking these ornaments of love with your daily existence, you can never have perception of the whole, therefore you will always be sad and when the end comes, you will still be groping in the darkness of your cell; you will have had nothing but halluncinations and a lot of empty words. But if you fall in love, now with these unique gifts, if you love your *kesh* now, the *kirpan* you wear, then, son as you grow up, you will not remain in your dungeon with its dark windows but will leave it and love the whole way of life. If you don't constantly have a passionate love for those presents of the Guru, then you are like a flower without fragrance, withered and lying in the dust, being crushed and kicked by every pedestrian. Only he can have love for God, who abandons his ego, forgets himself completely and thereby brings the state of creative consciousness. The 'me' the 'I' from its very birth is constantly building a barrier of knowledge around itself, around its actions and ultimately leads to isolation and despair. A life of the dead.

Knowledge is only a minor part of life, not the totality, and when it thus assumes all consuming significance, as it is now, then your life becomes artificial, an empty cup, from which man tries to escape, through superficial escapes with disastrous results. Knowledge is like a kerosene lamp on a dark night; it can illuminate only so long as it has fuel. Life is much vaster and deeper; it cannot be alive with the aid of an extinguishable lamp. Knowledge is essential to everyday existence, as money is to buy your food, but it cannot grasp the reality of love, of God, of loving. Love is not to be hookey in the net intelligence; if you use knowledge to grasp love, it will die as one fish dies out of water. Knowledge must be left behind for love to be. Burdened with mechanical learning you will never understand what is beauty, what is measurable. The light of knowledge cannot penetrate. The worship of knowledge is a ritualistic pilgrimage, which can never dissolve the contradictions and miseries of life. Mere knowledge, however earnestly learnt and cleverly assembled, will never resolve the meaning of the five Ks and to assume that it will, is to invite frustration and misery. You may know all about the working of earth and the functioning of the skies and still not be free from sorrow, envy and pain.

To know these gifts, to value truth, to be one with God, you must have claims to beliefs, no speculations '*Sochai soch noa hovai je sochai lakhvar*' (Guru Nanak), 'Mortal cannot comprehend Him by thought.' If you have gathered the knowledge of living, the knowledge itself becomes more important, not your living. If you want to understand these gifts, everything will come right. Live in them and there is understanding, '*hukmi andar sabh ko bahr hukam na koe. Nanak hukmi je bujhai ta haumai kahe na koe.*' (Guru Nanak), 'Nothing at all outside His will, abiding O Nanak, he who is aware of the Supreme will, never in his selfhood utters the boast: It is I'. The Supreme will has to live in the glory of these embellishments of our land, so shall it be.

These gifts of ours are not symbols of a religion, or compulsory rites of religion. The Sikh way of life is not to live on any set of rituals, formalism, talismans, penances, austerites, pilgrimages or symbols. The Sikhs were rebels against all this and more. The *Gurbani* abounds in hymns against ritualism and symbols. Guru Nanak Devji said in one of his compositions, 'Yoga lies not in wearing patched garments, nor in carrying a staff, nor in smearing one's body with ashes, nor does it lie in wearing earrings, nor in cutting one's hair, nor in playing on *singi*' (Suhi 1). Could anyone have said some thing more against the irrelevance of symbols? How strongly he felt against empty symbols may be gauged from these lines, 'With *tikka* (the sacred mark) on their forheads and *dhoti* wrapped around their loins and legs, they look pious, but in fact they are the world's butchers carrying daggers in their hands' (*Asa di Var*). The shallowness of ritualism and symbols was exposed thoroughly by Guru Gobind Singhji in the *Akal Ustat*:

Some worship but stocks and stones,
while others suspend the lingum from their necks.
Some look out for God in the East,
other in the West, to worship the dead;
All these are involved in a false show,
and they find not the Mystery, that is God.

After the victory in the battle of Bhangani, Guru Gobind Singhji blessed Pir Budhu Singh, with no treasures and no elephants, for his service, as was the custom of that time, but a *kirpan* and comb with some broken hair of his. These gifts are still preserved as sacred relics in the former princely state of Nabha. This very jewellery, he presented to all of us, inspite of the fact that our lives were not wrought in furnace of sacrifice—a jewellery which no craftsman, no intellectual, no jeweller is capable of imitating. These gifts of ours are the constellation of superconsciousness, the very essence of breath of God in us, of which our tress-knots are the spiritual crown of humanity.

Jaskirat, ask not from me, the significance, the value, power of our tress-knots, for I am incapable of describing it. In the meadows, dales and mountains of our tress-knots, the bliss of perennial joy flows; in the beautitude of our tress-knot, the owners are fired. In our mystical tress-knots, the insipid mankind is inspired in the holiness of our pristine pure tress-knots; the melting snow caps of the mountain peaks, wash away all sorrows; in our august tress-knots, the frenzied rain torrents pour; in the creativity of our transcendental tress-knots, his nakedness is robbed anew in the effulgence of these gifts.

Live in the eternal joy of your tress-knots and you will know what it is to be. Men collect the ashes of the departed soul and pray for him in the church and the temples and you want to discard, this living soul, this living temple! People build monuments for the dead, you want to uproot the living monuments the Guru gave to you. If you want it to disintegrate you may, but you shall forever be buried under it.

Love shall still come your way because you are one of the descendants of the ancient lore; you will still flex your muscles when the song is of your forefathers, but you would have converted the garden of the living into the weds of the dead. Soon, even his tears will dry as he tends new gardens. A time comes when no one knows of the long ruined monument. It passes back into the womb of agony and is possessed by the serpents, jackals and chameleons.

Jaskirat our five Ks are beyond the realm of rituals and symbols, they are the timeless ones. Can you and me enclose with our intellects what is not measurable? Can you and me enclose with or intellects what is not time? Can our constant hatred, anger and ugliness, lead us to the unknown? Do we have an instrument to gauge, what has no beginning and no end? Can the truth of these gifts be trapped in the cage of our logic? What we may capture by our mechanical knowledge and logic is superficial, never the essence of these presents. Many of us spiritedly respond to tranquillizers but living in love, needs no tranquillizers.

The beautiful, the loved can never be dissected and summed up. For these gifts, we can reach no conclusions, no morals and no judgements because they are not symbols but pieces of art. What would the cuckoo's song mean to you if you want to take down its notations and analyse them? What would your mother be for you if you want to know her by analysis? Only a biological skeleton for procreation. You have so much entrapped yourself in a net of words, of speculations that the feeling itself, which is the only thing that is deep and vital in us, is lost. The significance or the insignificance of these gifts is not important. The highest art in life is to be beautiful. And these gifts are the force that create the beautiful, the artist, in us. It is one in a million, who has the beauty of these ornaments.

The *kesh*, the *kachha*, the *kara*, the *kangha* and the *kirpan*, and the gifts have been chiselled out for the Khalsa, by the divine artist. These are the gifts, endowed to us for every, by the Divine Bridegroom, on the day of our marriage to him, on Baisakhi, in 1699, at Anandpur Sahib (The City of Bliss). They are the true embodiments of art and any one looking at them, can have his bosom full of meaning, ecstacy, inspiration, love, joy. What more can we ask for? In them we have the treasure, mines, in them is the beauty and we are so ignorant of it. We the cosmic brides will carry his gifts of love, in honour, purity and splendid glory, and our love will blossom in all climates, in all times and in continents.

May the blessing of *Waheguruji* be with you forever.

Your loving father
Harcharan Singh

Three months after receiving this letter from his father Jaskirat Singh felt that the time had come to keep his vow to his father. Bathed in the harmony, melody and fragrance of a new dawn, he travelled to Shri Anandpur Sahib on 18 October 1977, and affirmed his love for the Guru Sahib, by taking *khande ka amrit*, at Gurudwara Keshgarh Sahib—the birth place of the Khalsa. In keeping with the Khalsa tradition, he accepted Guru Gobind Singh as his spiritual Father and Mata Sahib Kaur as his spiritual Mother, and Anandpur Sahib as place of his new birth.

A Letter from a Son to his Father

Respected Father

Sat Siri Akal

Your enquiry from a third party in this country as to whether I was still wearing my turban and hair after living here for five years, has prompted me to write this letter in addition to the regular family correspondence.

It was nice of you to enquire about my welfare. It, however, reflected a typical parental worry by numerous people who summarize Sikhism in a beard and a turban alone and not in the fundamental principles. Having been born and brought up in a Sikh family was the reason I was a Sikh before leaving India, but the reason now is some what different. Now it is because I have decided to be a Sikh. This is how it all happened.

During my second year here, I asked myself a question: What is Sikhism and why am I a Sikh? With an in-built curiosity and a mind oriented for scientific research, I was unwilling to accept the idea that I will remain a Sikh simply because I was born in a Sikh family. As you know recitation from *Guru Granth Sahib* was a daily ritual in our home and still is, but no one ever mentioned that I should learn Punjabi. The result is that till now I can't write our script and whatever reading practice I have, is from reading mother's letters all these years. At home, I was told to and I did memorize *Japji*, but no one told me what it meant. I recall that belief in horoscopes and fasting was common in our family and now I wonder how little of the Sikh philosophy did we incorporate in our daily life. With a past such as this, my above questions were bound to appear sooner or later.

Where should I go in search of more facts about the history and heritage of the Sikh in this foreign land? This was my next question. I started by looking under the word 'Sikh' in the reference catalogue of the library of a big university. To my surprise I found a treasure.

---

* Reproduced from *A Spur to the Sikh Youth*. The Sikh Missionary Society, Gravesend, UK, 1972.

The need to know more about myself was so great and urgent that everyday's delay amounted to a sense of guilt and unfulfilment. With a full academic load, I started on my 'search'.

I started off with the recently published *History of the Sikhs*, vol. I, by Kushwant Singh. It was very informative and translations of the holy writings at the end of the book were most valuable. For the first time I understood *Japji* and the *Mool-Mantra* which defined the Sikh (concept of) God. I discovered great rationalism and maturity in the words, 'There is but One God, who is all Truth, the Creator, without fear and enmity, Immortal, Unborn, Self-existent. The True One was in the beginning, is now also and shall be in future too.'

Such a description of God did away with controversial and naive ideas like, the colour of his skin, his place of birth, and numerous other attributes bestowed by man. But the most significant thing I found was that the definition of *Akal Purakh* did away with the immature and egotistical human practice of casting God in the human grab, making Him subject to the laws of life and death, a form imperfect by definition and improper for the Almighty. Evolution of such a concept as written in the *Mool-Mantra*, shows unusual maturity in the earliest stages of the development of Sikhism.

Then came Khushwant Singh's second volume of the *History of the Sikhs*, published in 1966 by the Princeton University Press. I was lucky to find the *Heritage of the Sikhs* by Harbans Singh, published in 1964 in India. I learnt a lot from this book. Before that, I was unaware of the Sikh-English relations, the Singh Sabha and the Gurdwara Movement, the account of Chief Khalsa Diwan and other happenings in the past 120 years or so. One by one I read the works of Cunningham, Macauliffe, Kohli, Bannerji, Ganda Singh, Gopal Singh and others including the biography of Maharaja Ranjit Singh by Fakir Syed Waheedudeen published in 1965 from Pakistan. Regularly I read *The Sikh Review* from Calcutta and *The Sikh Courier* form London.

Well you may ask, 'What happened from all this study you did?' I think I have an answer. In India, I was a Sikh, true, but an inactive one, unaware of the rich heritage that covered five centuries before me, and just a Sikh in name. Now I am a Sikh, but not the same that I was in India. There I was a Sikh because I was born in a Sikh family. At this age and stage, I am a Sikh because I want to be one and so will I remain primarily because of my appreciation of what our religion stood for and stands for.

Have I cut my hair or will I? Part of this was the question you secretly asked someone else. I will not think of cutting my hair any more than removing my finger, or arm, or leg from my body. The hair, besides being a cherished gift from Guru Gobind Singh, is an integral part of me. How could I barter myself to suit some immature minds? Principles of Sikhism are sound enough to enable a Sikh to meet others on his own ground.

Although there is a lot of quibbling on religion even among people worshipping the same God in this country, America is basically tolerant to individual characteristics. My five years have not seen a single case where I felt bad or odd because I wear a turban. I know that the sight of a Sikh male catches immediate attention, or comment or stares. This is not an American characteristic, but a human one. Man is always curious, cautious, and perhaps suspicious of things or persons new in his environment. I remember how we used to stare at the Christian monks and nuns in their long 'peculiar' garbs when we were small.

Some Sikhs I know who came to this country shaved off their hair after varying periods of stay. One of them, a good friend of mine, removed his hair in the second year. One day when I asked him casually about the change, he said, 'I used to feel warm and uncomfortable in my office because of hair and turban.' I really had a big laugh because this boy had spent twenty years living in Rajasthan (India), without feeling uncomfortable and here in an air-conditioned office 'he felt uncomfortable'.

There are several cases like the one just mentioned because most of such people have an inferiority complex or lack in self-confidence. This is most likely due to their lack of knowledge about themselves and what they stand for. They are immature to the extent that they find it necessary to remould themselves in the shape of the majority they live with.

I find Sikhism more than just the outer appearance of a Sikh. If this were not so, I would not be writing this letter since I don't think Sikhs would have survived that long. There is a very fine example here. A gentleman I know is what we call a *Sahajdhari*. But he is one of the strongest moving force behind Sikh gatherings and celebrations in Chicago area. He travels several hundred miles to attend the monthly *kirtan* in Chicago (USA). He is certainly a good Sikh.

My case is typical of an urban Sikh boy of India. He takes religion for granted. His family makes little attempt to make him more than a Sikh in appearance. Unfortunately, every boy who has been brought up the way I was, will not have easy access to books and other media on the subject because books are so expensive. But I sincerely hope that parents, schools and other organizations in India will leave no stone unturned to educate their children, students, and members.

Here is a noble project for Shiromani Gurdwara Parbandhak Committee.

Sikhism will bloom to full potential only when the Sikhs understand the foundation of their very existence and live as they are supposed to. Sikhism is not a passive religion. Sikhs cannot afford to be passive. There are a lot of vultures all over the place.

So, here I am; a Sikh by choice. I cannot call myself a real Sikh because I have recently discovered myself. But one thing is sure, I have found the way.

With best regards to all at home.

Your loving son
Veer Singh

Contributors

SARDUL SINGH CAVEESHAR was a prominent Akali Leader.

VINAY LAL teaches in the Department of History, University of California, Los Angles, USA.

W.H. MCLEOD is Professor of History, University of Dunedin, New Zealand.

J.S. NEKI is an eminent poet, writer and former Director of PGI and Consultant, WHO.

BAWA HARKISHAN SINGH was Principal, G.N. College, Gujranwala (Pakistan).

BHAGAT SINGH is a former Session Judge.

BHAI JODH SINGH was Principal of Khalsa College, Amritsar and late Vice-Chancellor of Punjabi University, Patiala.

GANDA SINGH was Director of Department of Punjab Historical Studies, Punjabi University, Patiala.

GURMUKH NIHAL SINGH was Vice-Chancellor of University of Delhi, General Secretary of Guru Nanak Foundation and late Governor of Rajasthan.

I.J. SINGH is Professor and Coordinator, Anatomical Sciences, New York University, New York.

TEJA SINGH was Principal of Government Mahendra College, Patiala.

TRILOCHAN SINGH was an eminent Sikh scholar.

J.P.S. UBEROI is Professor of Sociology, Delhi School of Social Work, University of Delhi, Delhi.

P.M. WYLAM is a former Member of the Editorial Advisory Board, *The Sikh Review*, Calcutta.

Index

Jatadhari jogis 70-1
Jews 48
Jews swore by hair 48
Jodh Singh, Bhai 11
Joga Singh, Bhai 62
Jogi (yogi) 16, 69, 71; initiation of 69; vows of 69
Judaism 48
Jung, C.G. 147

Kachha 31-2, 36; trousers of chastity 36; essentials 43, 62, 81, 85; worn for perpetual readiness 62; promotes chastity 62; protective garment 62; a garment for the loin and thighs 72; is a satorial symbol signifying manly reserves in commitment to the procreative world as against renouncing it 72, 87; of continence 75
Kachhahra 101
Kakar 'K' 41, 85
Kalal, Guru ka Lal 152
Kalu, Mehta 96
Kangha 31-2, 41-2, 52; comb of purity 36; essentials 43, 71, 85; symbolizes cleanliness 86
Kanphata 69-70
Kara 31-2, 60, 63, 92; made of steel 61; physical utility 61; symbolizes determination 61; a sort of handcuff 61; worn by Sahajdharis 61; iron bangle as a mark of sohag 61; binds the Sikh to his religion to the Khalsa and to Sikh brothers 81; a steel bangle symbolizes for the Sikh a just and lawful life of self-discipline and self-control 87; handcuff of honesty 36; essentials 43
Kartarpur 96
Kashmir 40
Kaur 78, 98, 110
Kes, Kesh or hair 25, 27-8, 31-2, 36, 42; medical properties 27; a help to organization 28; indispensable 39; long hair and long beard 41; first token of Sikh faith 42; essential 43; chief symbol 57; emblem of virtue 35; biological significance 58; at once natural 59; test of disciples courage 59; promotes group consciousness 65; most cherished and distinctive signs of an individual's membership of the Sikh Panth 65; distinct from jata 72; unshorn hair also signify manliness, virility, courage and dignity 86; symbolizes for the Sikhs a life of spiritual devotion (bhakti) and of strength (shakti) of conviction of courage and fortitude 86; seem to have primary position 87
Keshav 86
Keshdhari Sikhs 59, 98
Keshgarh Sahib Gurdwara 162
Khalistan 118, 129, 130
Khalsa 13, 41; tercentenary of creation of 13; is always on duty 36; his battle is never ending one 36; uniform helps to remind of their duty 37; hair and beard as part of the personality 42; also known as Singhs 42; was created for service to mankind 58; militant 59; brotherhood 53; ideals 53; rules for guidance 78, 88; defination (by Guru Gobind Singh) 78; Khalsa Sikh children 125-6; Khalsa Sikh studies 124; has a central vital role to play in the life of the Panth 95; establishment of 96, 99, 102-3; the Sikh with his external uniform and symbols is a Khalsa, a soldier in the army of God 91; a life of militant devotion to their faith 110; comprises only those who have taken initiation 102; in common usage however Khalsa is extended to cover Keshdhari Sikhs also 102; symbols denoting solidarity and militancy in the name of the faith 113
Khalsa Sikhs 78, 101, 103, 124, 125
Khande da Amrit 40, 162
Khuda 156
Khyber Pass 99-100

Sikh separatism 129
Sikh soldiers 101
Sikh studies 65
Sikh symbols functional 90, 91
Sikh Tract Society, Lahore 28
Sikhism 11, 13, 15, 17, 23, 27; spirit of 25, 29, 71, 78; aim is disciplined emotion and enlightened sentiment 27; religion of the spirit 33; duty enjoined by 43; devotion to 43; believes in life affirming view of life 47, 63, 65, 68, 75; a religious brotherhood 71; spirit of affirmation 72; principles of 79; rules of 78; a completely separate religion 99, 102, 166
Sikhs 11-12, 15, 17, 19, 21-3, 41; at home 27; inspired 31; five symbols of 36; Massacre of 42; preferred to lay down their lives 42; played the part as neutrals 43; united brotherhood character 61; law abiding citizens 127
Simla hills 73
Singh/Singhs 41-3, 59, 97; members of civic guard 61; common surname 78
Singh Sabha movement 97, 98; Singh Sabhas 113, 164
Śiva's tresses 51
Soldier(s) 11, 18; uniform 29; true 35; force of character 35; inner uniform and outward uniform 36; military uniform 36
South Asia 118
South-East Asia 99
Soviet Union 62
Spiritual doctrines 23
Sri Lanka 90
Sri Sahib 88
Stockton Gurdwara 118
Sūfī darvesh 52
Sūfī saints 54
Sultanpur Lodhi 96
Sun Yat-sen's movement 62, 67
Supreme Being 151
Supreme Court 124, 126, 132
Surrey School District 120

Sutak 23
Svadharma 53
Sword, double-edged 10; for defending the weak 36
'Sword of God' 86
Symbol(s) 9, 16-17, 20, 32, 61, 65; definition 9; origin 9; religious 9-10; of highest personality 21; as sacrosant 29; question of 29; Indians worship God through the use of 29; mere symbols 29; representing God 29; of a Sikh remind him of his duties 30; degenerate into mere form 30; unquestioning reverence 32; external 32; five 36; of Sikh faith 39, 119; symbols came to signify the distinctive identity and collective aspirations of the Sikh people 88; being the gift of the Guru 88; signify the Sikhs love for their Guru as also his for them 88; organizational, ethical and spiritual values 64; unique mystical 77; infuse spirit of oneness 80; serve the purpose of a uniform 80; vital 105; functional 91; Guru ordained them 91; are embodiment of history 92; are seen in every act of faith 89; cannot be invented at will, they grow out of the collective consciousness of people 89; their majesty and power lies in their symbolic character 89; we are wedded women of God they are the wedding gifts from the Bridegroom 154
Symbolic, language script 29
Symbolism 47

Taboo, proscriptive (Kurehit) 39, 65, 87
Tagore, Rabindranath 58, 157
Taiping rebellion 62, 67
Talvandi 96
Tankhahnama 40
Tankhaia 25
Tantric yogi 86
Taru Singh, Bhai 31-2, 155-8
Tat Khalsa 98